Airbnb Startup Guide

Building Wealth with Airbnb

How I Used Airbnb to Create a Lucrative Income

I0491496

By

Spencer Cooper

Published by:

Streets of Dream
Press

Streets of Dream Press

Cover & Interior designed

By

Renee Leadsman

First Edition

Contents

Introduction

It is no news that the past two decades have been fraught with several global financial challenges. These rollercoaster events began with the 2008 financial crisis, which brought the worst fiscal cataclysm. In actuality, this encounter didn't pale in comparison to the Great Depression of 1929 and demeaned the immense efforts of the U.S Department of the Treasury and the Federal Reserve, even creating a ripple effect worldwide. Unemployment hovered above 9% as many businesses shut down and individuals lost their jobs. The real estate, alongside other sectors, took a major hit.

Fast-forward to 2020, the novel Coronavirus Disease 2019 (COVID-19) shook the global sphere, sending negative economic and life-threatening shockwaves that left more than a million people dead and businesses inactive. There are growing concerns worldwide about the future and its hope for mankind. Even worse, this looming global recession could be the ugliest of all times as everyone braces for what is to come. There are no sustainable jobs anymore. As such, most people are creating more channels to earn additional income streams.

Delving into the white-collar environment, many individuals slave themselves to earn meager incomes that are insufficient to cater to their daily livelihoods. Undoubtedly, they devote their resources, including their will, time, creativity, and strength, to meet daily work tasks. Although such inputs contribute immensely to the business growth and expansion of the firms and companies these individuals work for and the society at large, they benefit little in return. And the pensions they thought were once secure are nothing more than a wishy-washy enterprise, incapable of giving them a valued post-retirement lifestyle.

As bone-chilling as it sounds, such workaholics have several dependents, which increases the level of responsibility they bear. The overwhelming pressure to make ends meet has created adverse effects, like depression, avoidant personality disorder, high-stress levels, persistent suicidal thought patterns, destabilized relationships, and even suicide. It becomes obvious that the solution to these problems is to build wealth through various tested and trusted income streams, one of which includes Airbnb.

The comprehensive guide "Building Wealth with Airbnb" shows you how to create a passive income-generating avenue by utilizing the Airbnb platform. It is a well-detailed, action-packed book with informative steps that will help you smash through the reef of unemployment and unprofitable 9-5 experience, making you financially independent in the process. In other words, you can create the ideal lifestyle you want without breaking a sweat. Gone are the days when people had to work hard, living from hand to mouth.

Wealth generation is the holy grail that can release you from the rat race and set you on the path of becoming financially free for life. Based on many financial experts' reports, a true economic self-sufficient individual earns from more than five income streams. So, even if you haven't had any other avenue from your daily white-collar job, Airbnb can be your first step to creating generational wealth in these trying times. What does this guide cover?

An introduction to the world of Airbnb, including its history and specific terms you should know.

The moving parts that make this platform an instrumental support system to real estate.

How you can join profitable Airbnb listers to create a long-lasting passive income.

Strategies and hacks that can make you run a successful Airbnb business, even with little money.

Legal factors to consider, including property tax.

Resolving problems and handling reviews.

Related jobs to engage in that can add multiple income streams to your portfolio.

In recent times, several drastic economic trends have created a global shift that can make millionaires and billionaires and also increase the global poverty rate. Preparing ahead will save you from the looming financial holocaust that may wipe out millions of household incomes. The action plans in this book will help you work your way towards becoming financially independent. You can also refer this guide to your family and friends, opening them up to a world they didn't know existed. If you are ready to take the first step to build wealth, let's proceed on this fascinating journey.

Financial freedom is not a term that should be restricted to the millionaires and billionaires of this world. It is a must-have for anyone keen on becoming self-reliant. You don't have to be dependent on your boss to live the life you deserve. However, even though everyone aspires to be wealthy, only a handful truly achieve this goal. How factual is this statement? Statistics from the 2019 Credit Suisse Global Wealth Report shows that the richest 1% controls 44% of global wealth.

These are individuals with a net worth exceeding $1 million. Sadly, more than 55% of the world's population controls less than 2% of global wealth, less than $10,000. But it gets worse from here. About 0.002% of the population worldwide dominates 7.2% of the world's wealth, sitting above the $30-million benchmark, with about 0.022% owning almost 5% share of wealth ($5 million to $29.9 million), and 0.217%

overseeing 9.4% ($1 million to $4.9 million).

Interestingly, the world's 10 richest billionaires have a combined net worth of $801 billion, which has increased tremendously during this pandemic. In actuality, Statista claims that these individuals have gained $1 trillion since March 2020. A startling example is that of Elon Musk, Tesla and SpaceX CEO, who gained a staggering $101.6 billion, shooting him from $24.6 billion to $126.2 billion. As such, he is the second richest man in the world, next to Jeff Bezos.

Taking these statistics into account, it becomes glaring that there is a need to generate wealth to survive the looming financial doom. Believe me when I state that the world isn't going to get any better, especially for those clinging to their 9-5 monthly paychecks. Besides, job insecurity is the order of the day. How long do you think you could last in your workplace? What happens when you wake up one morning to realize that your boss has relieved you of your duty. It's more catastrophic for those that have exceeded the job market age requirement. They would have to settle for something less or depend on family and friends for survival.

In today's world, it is risky to have one source of income. However, other avenues like the stocks market, Forex, bunds, mutual funds, and the likes don't guarantee you a "safe" and high-rewarding financial safety net to protect you during rainy days. Here's what you should know (and I have witnessed this first-hand), most of the wealthy folks in our society, among other investments, have one that is guaranteed to create generational wealth. And what is that? You may have guessed right – real estate. However, this industry is fraught with several technicalities and challenges, capable of leaving you mentally drained. Above all, it is a capital-intensive field.

But as the world progresses, you don't have to conform to the traditional standards to earn a living from real estate. In actuality, you don't even have to own a property or have millions of dollars stashed in your bank account to succeed in this sector. I am living proof that this multi-dollar industry can generate long--term wealth for anyone who looks in the right direction. Who says you need a home to get started when you can achieve the same goals with Airbnb? I presume this subject has piqued your interest. Hence, without further ado, let's delve into this amazing world.

Chapter 1: My Personal Journey to Growing a Successful Airbnb Business

What comes to mind when the term "Airbnb" pops up now and then? Is it a rental platform that has homeowners smiling to the bank at the end of the month? Airbnb does not just entail listing a part of your apartment for a couple of weeks. It goes beyond tourists, holidaymakers, and even foreign exchange students booking your home for a specific period. I will state that Airbnb is a business solution that meets several needs, including those that transcend real estate. This digital platform is not another commercial spin-off from the traditional hotels and guest houses – it is so much more.

In actuality, many individuals from around the world have provided solutions that bridge the gap between renters and homeowners through Airbnb. It is a valuable system that doesn't focus solely on renting houses. On the contrary, it stands out from the rest by providing a home-away-from-home experience for people from all walks of life. With this ideology in mind, this single, modest rental business turned $31 billion company has spread its tentacles in 167 countries. What makes Airbnb unique? It gives travelers and tourists the first-hand experience of a local. As I stated before, it transcends rentals as hosts can provide renters with tours, events, and over experiences that make their stay memorable.

The fact remains that humanity will need shelter, which is one of three necessities of life. The ultra-wealthy understand this factor and capitalize on it to resolve the challenges faced by people in need of them. To create an environment that promotes financial freedom, you have to offer solutions that address people's concerns. Airbnb offers that platform, in turn, creating a passive income for hosts. This online marketplace proffers a win-win solution, where renters get an awesome home-like experience, and Airbnb hosts expand their financial portfolio. No doubt, tourists and holidaymakers want to get the best travel experience, regardless of their destination.

Unlike the hotels and motels, Airbnb homes provide the right details that meet such individuals' lifestyles and preferences. These customized provisions make you feel that the homeowner had you in mind when creating them. On the other hand, if the amenities available are out of place, you may feel neglected. Hence, Airbnb is not solely about the rental, even though that counts; it focuses on taking away the home-sick feeling people get when they move to a different location.

I had not considered these intricate factors when I started in June 2012 – this was when Airbnb announced its 10 millionth booking. Before this time, I ran a laundromat while maintaining my nine to five job as a lead customer service representative with a mid-sized company in Morristown, New Jersey. With an annual take-home pay of $50,000 and a business that earned me $48,000, I felt satisfied with my lifestyle. However, the bills kept skyrocketing, including my

$1,300 per month mortgage. As such, it was a priority to create more avenues to make money.

Besides, financial freedom is everything to me. I needed an additional income stream that paid me passively – one that could still run smoothly if I weren't there. This desire led to Airbnb. At this time, my home was a liability, feeding off of my earnings every month. I needed something to offset part of my bills and give me more money to invest in other things. Having thought about my apartment and the need to rent it out on some days while I was away at my parents' place, I struck a deal with my mortgage lender. That is how my Airbnb journey began.

In reality, the early stage of my Airbnb journey was a rough one. Unlike the amount of information available today, which anyone can harness to begin any business, I knew nothing about providing an optimum lodging experience. To me, it was all about renting my space to individuals who came from other states to see top tourist spots in New Jersey. And here is what happened. Even though my apartment had tasteful furnishing, guests still complained about feeling homesick and a bit out of place.

April 2013 (almost a year after I started Airbnb) brought

about a tough time for me. My laundromat business had dwindled in sales, fetching only $1,200 on average per month. The pressure at work doubled. My monthly bills weren't idle either, as they shot through the roof. At this point, I considered quitting Airbnb as there was little or less flowing in for me. Besides, those who had visited didn't consider coming back. It seemed I had plunged into a downward spiral, and no one was going to save me. Three months fleeted by and still nothing – no progress.

On the 3rd of September, I was driving down 1022 Lafayette Street, Cape May, when I stopped to admire the houses that nestled on either side of the road. Out of the blues, a thought popped up, "Wait a sec – anyone would love to live here." Being there gave me a home-like feeling, which made my mind drift towards my apartment. And then another thought, "Why drooling over these homes when I can replicate them in mine?" And then, it hit me like a thunderbolt. I had an idea – turning my house into a home. With $154,000 saved up the last three years, the project commenced.

It went on for almost two months. On the first of December, my home had taken a new disposition – one, my guests would not resist. I had invited my family over for Christmas and could still picture the warm and astonishing looks on their faces when they stepped into my apartment.

It was a "home sweet home." With that completed, it was time to revamp my listing. This time around, no one was going to say no to my home. And sure, that happened. In less than three weeks, I received an offer from a newlywed couple who were in NJ to experience the amazing sight the state offered. I could tell that they had enjoyed their stay at my place because they came back six months later.

In a year, I had hosted five individuals, aside from the amazing couples. At this point, my yearly earning hovered a little above $9,000. It was a fresh start for me – an exhilarating feeling I couldn't let go of for one second. I had created an additional income stream, which was my third. The following, I thought of attaining more. My laundromat business was still struggling. However, an idea struck me on New Year's Eve of 2014, "Why don't I provide my guests with value-added services to make their stay more memorable?" With that, my Airbnb business took a pivotal motion the following year.

By the end of 2015, I had netted $21,000. Additionally, my laundromat generated $65,000. My total income for the year was $136,000. I could afford to quit my job and still survive. However, I was not about that life as there was much to do. Fortunately, my years of work and learning paid off. Fast-forward to today, I earn over $56,000 a year from Airbnb alone. With more than 15 stays a year and increasing, I have achieved the status of a super host in the Airbnb world. But that's not the topping. My guests are highly satisfied with my apartment, which they consider their second home.

Here is a secret worth knowing about Airbnb and what makes the brand unique. Guests desire to take their identities along wherever they go. They want optimum hospitality that makes them forget their homes. Unfortunately, most hosts don't understand this – I didn't know at first. It is easy for anyone to conclude that an apartment is what it is – an "apartment." However, one thing they forget is that a home has an identity, which reflects that of the occupant.

Once this is out of place, it becomes a house. In the Airbnb industry, it isn't about you and what you want; this is another mistake I made when starting this business. I assumed my taste reflected everyone's desire. But this threw my guests' identities out of the window – something no one would want. Once I fixed that missing piece, the picture became complete. In listing your space, you should ensure that you are not missing the element of "customization."

What do I mean by this? How is your apartment designed to meet the cultural values and background of your guests? And I am not talking about renovating your home every time a visitor leaves to suit the next person. What design elements are you considering that will give your property a homey vibe? Sometimes, a little touch here and there may be all you need to transform your pallid studio apartment into a five-star live-in residence.

With the right approach, you can turn your space into a hosting platform that easily accommodates people from all walks of life and cultural backgrounds. Guests can step into your home and stay for as long as they want without feeling homesick.

There is nothing as pleasant hearing them say, "I love this place," "Yes, this feels like home," "Honey, I don't want to leave." At that point, you know you've hit the nail on the head. Do not see your residence as a rental space, or else, it makes yours no different from the shabby motel down the street. Hospitality and diversity are the watchwords here.

Chapter 2: Airbnb Terminology Worth Knowing

Airbnb is not just an online marketplace; it is an economic revolution that has transformed the lives of millions of individuals across the globe. Most people have had to quit their white-collar jobs to run this enterprise full time. And even those that still run their 9-to-5 can still boast of a passive income. The fact remains that we have needs. The bills are not going to sort out themselves. You need an added avenue that can meet your utility bills, mortgage, auto loan, shopping, and many more.

Like I stated before, having one source of income is risky as you are a step away from unemployment. It is essential to create other sources that generate additional revenue. Airbnb is an ideal start. However, it doesn't come on a platter of gold. As with other investments, you need to understand specific aspects, including terms used in this industry. Here are some words you will come across, not only in Airbnb but also in real estate.

A

Accessible Vacation Rental: This refers to a property modified by its owner or a real estate agent to accommodate persons with disabilities.

Advance Payment: It is a part of the entire rental fee paid upfront by guests for their lodge.

Advertised Price: It is the displayed price per night of rental space.

Amenities: These are the functional features a property possesses. They could include Wi-Fi and air conditioners.

Amenity Fee: It is an added charge that comes with using specific amenities, such as laundry services, gym provision, and many more.

American Society of Home Inspectors (ASHI): A non-profit association that comprises home inspection professionals who incorporate and monitor standards for properties in North America.

Availability Calendar: This is a virtual calendar that displays the availability of a property for rent.

Available Nights: It depicts the availability of a property for booking for a specific number of nights per year. Other times, the owner may reside in it for a given period.

Average Daily Rate (ADR): Also known as the average room rate, this shows the average rental income of a single payment made for a stay under a specific timeframe. It is a widely known term in the hospitality industry. To arrive at the exact figure, property owners take into account the average revenue generated and divide it by the number of booked rooms.

Average Length of Stay (ALOS): It shows the average number of nights spent on a property within a given period, which can range from a week to a year.

Average Rate Index (ARI): Used to determine the success rate of a property rental, ARI compares the average daily rate of an individual's rental property with that of other competitors. As such, owners can tell if they should increase or decrease room rental fees.

B

Back-to-Back Booking: A situation where another guest lodge in an apartment on the same day the previous occupant checks out.

Bartered Services: Lodging in a home in exchange for products and services, including repairs and maintenance.

Best Available Rate (BAR): It is the minimum, unrestricted rate available for booking. Additionally, it is not fixed.

Best Rate Guarantee: The assurance of a rate being the best a guest can find on any property.

Billboard Effect: Also known as window shopping, it is a theory, which states that properties listed on several agency sites and portals will get more direct bookings due to increased visibility.

Booking: It is the act of acquiring temporary ownership of a rental property for a specific period. Another term for this is "Reservation."

Booking Confirmation: A notification received when a guest books a rental space. It confirms that a successful booking and other aspects, including reference details, contract, and rules.

Booking Curve: This is a graphical tool that depicts bookings over a specified timeframe. It helps with decision making on property availability and rental rate adjustment.

Booking Engine: It is any software or application embedded on a lodging website to help guests process bookings and payments.

Booking Fee: A charge deducted by agencies or lodging sites to process guests' bookings.

Booking Policy: It refers to the terms and conditions of bookings, including payment deadlines, the incurrence of damages, and booking cancellations.

Booking Request: A reservation means through which guests can check-in for the availability of rental space and get approval before making payments.

Break-Even Point: It is a timeline that shows when investment in a property will yield enough returns to cover overhead costs.

Broom Clean: It defines the pristine state of a home or rental property.

C

Call-to-Action (CTA): This is a prompt that notifies online visitors or users to take specific action related to their visits. It could be a button or hyperlink with displays, like "Check-In Here" or "Book Now."

Cancellation Fee: It is a charge processed for canceling reservations after a deadline.

Cancellation Policy: A documentation explaining the rules concerning the cancellation of rental reservations or bookings.

Changeover Days: It defines certain days of the week when bookings can begin and end.

Channels: These are listing sites that showcase properties and allow owners to run them through a channel management software.

Channel Fee: It is a commission charged by a third-party agent for allowing owners to list their properties on a listing website.

Check-In: It defines the process by which a guest is formally registered on a property for their stay.

Check-Out: It is the process by which a guest leaves a property once their stay expires.

Cleaning Fee: It is a one-time fee that guests pay to property hosts to cover the cleaning cost once they check-out.

Co-Host: This is an Airbnb feature that allows a property owner to assign a co-host (one the owner knows already) to an Airbnb account. The co-host oversees the affairs of the property and guests.

Comparative Market Analysis (CMA): This is a report that shows details of other properties comparable to a specific home, which helps provide its accurate market value.

Competitive Set: It defines a collection of properties that are in direct competition with a particular property due to similarities in design, price, and target audience. Owners of these properties can compare one another's performance to make decisions that promote their rental businesses.

Complex: It is a building equipped with several rental units and often overseen by a vacation rental manager or a homeowners' association (HOA).

Cosmetic Upgrades: They refer to specific features applied to augment the aesthetics and value of a home. They may include new installations, fresh paintings, or added amenities.

D

Damage Deposit: It is a refundable amount a property owner charges a guest alongside the booking cost, which can be used to repair any damage incurred during the stay. Whereby there is none, the property owner refunds the money. Damage deposit, also known as a security deposit or breakage deposit, is generally around 10% of the rental fee or $200.

Damage Protection Insurance: It is a one-time rental insurance policy a guest purchases during bookings, which is an alternative to a damage deposit. It may cost between $50 to $100 per stay.

Damage Waiver Fee: This is a one-time non-refundable charge some property owners take from guests instead of a damage deposit. It can range from $25 to $100 per stay.

Deeded Access: It is a legal document granting a buyer access to a specific property. For instance, if you acquire a home that is in proximity to the ocean but not directly situated on the beach. Your property may come with deeded access through a mapped-out area to enjoy an ocean view.

Default Rate: It is the standard rental rate that applies to the property during working/business days or off-season periods.

Deposit Refund: A process through which a host returns a damage deposit, provided the property is in the same condition after checking out.

Depth of Inventory: A group of similar properties available for rent in a location.

Direct Booking: The act of reserving a rental space directly on a property owner or vacation rental manager's website.

Distribution Channel: This describes third-party websites where property owners can list their homes. They include Airbnb, Vrbo, Booking.com, and many more.

Domain Name: It is the address of a website name, which online visitors can use to access the site.

Double Booking: It is a situation where a rental space with an existing booking gets an additional reservation.

Down Payment: It refers to a partial payment (a percentage of the total booking fee) made to secure a rental space.

E

Equity: It is the amount derived by removing the mortgage owed on a property from its fair market value, which, in other words, is the financial interest the owner has to pay.

Eviction: It is the legal ejection of an occupant from a property.

Expenses: Money spent to cater to specific items. In real estate, expenses may include mortgage, insurance, property supplies, cleaning, maintenance, repairs, advertising costs, and many more.

F

Fair Housing Act: Also known as the 1968 Fair Housing Act, is a term that property owners and renters will come across often. It is a U.S. federal act that protects renters or buyers from discrimination directed at an individual's color, race, sex, religion, national origin, familial status, or handicap.

Fair Market Value (FMV): It reflects the market value of a property, which an informed buyer is willing to pay an owner in the market.

Fixed-Rate/Fixed-Term Mortgage: It is a mortgage that comes with a fixed interest rate within an agreed timeframe.

Fixer-Uppers: A property that requires maintenance to improve its aesthetics and value, even though it can still accommodate a renter or buyer. Properties of this category generally come with a low-price offer.

Flood Insurance: An insurance policy that protects a property value in the advent of flooding. In flood-prone areas, this coverage is a must-have.

FSBO (For Sale by Owner): A situation where a property owner decides to sell a home without a listing agent or company.

G

Gaps: This is a timeline that shows when properties are free of bookings.

Gross Booking Revenue: This is the sum of transaction retail values on bookings.

Guest Experience: A spin-off of the term customer experience, used to show each phase of a guest's overall feeling and encounter with a brand's service, starting with the first interaction all through to the individual's check-out, and even beyond that.

Guest Fee: Also known as a service fee, it is an additional charge paid by a guest for additional services, such as a cleaning fee.

Guest Screening: It is an evaluation process that gives property managers and owners an idea of their guests before they are allowed on the property.

H

Homeowners' Association (HOA): It is an association

responsible for implementing and enforcing specific rules on property owners and renters in a location. This group oversees the maintenance and financial management of the real estate.

Homeowners Insurance: This is a type of insurance policy that covers property loss and damages, which includes accidents.

House Rules: These are rules set by a property owner, a manager, or a host to notify guests of what is expected from them.

I

Inquiry: The process by which a potential renter or guest seeks information on a property.

Installment: It refers to a lump-sum payment being broken into smaller parts to be paid within an agreed timeframe.

Instant Booking: This is a type of reservation that allows guests to secure a rental space without the owner's, manager's, or host's approval. They don't have to contact the owner before selecting a date or a particular rental unit and making payments.

Inventory: This is a portfolio of real estate a property manager showcases to renters, guests, or buyers.

Investment Property Loan: It is a loan procured to fund a commercial property construction.

Invoice: It is a document that serves as proof of payment for a booking or rent. Additionally, guests can monitor their expenses using this financial statement.

K

Key Exchange Solution: This is any software that processes the allocation and collection of room keys.

Keyless Entry: A solution that enables guests to access their booked rooms without the use of keys. One of these solutions is the use of temporary passcodes.

Key Performance Indicators (KPIs): These are computable parameters used to monitor a business performance within a specific timeframe. In the rental industry, KPIs show the property's success in the areas of conversion rate, occupancy rate, and more.

L

Length of Stay (LOS) Pricing: This approach enables owners to provide guests and renters with discounts for longer stays.

Licenses: These are legal documents that may be required of a homeowner before the approval of a rental service.

Listing: It showcases a property profile on a listing or property agency site and is not limited to the property title, location, description, pricing, images, and other details.

Listing Site: It is a third-party agency website that shows a list of properties advertised. Another term for this is "Online Travel Agency (OTA)," and examples include Airbnb and Vrbo.

Lockbox: A secured compartment that houses the keys to a homeowner's property. Often, to access this safe, a code combination is required.

Low Season: It defines the period of a year when there is less travel, culminating in fewer bookings. During this time, rental managers and owners lower their rates to attract renters. It is also known as an off-peak season.

Luxury Property: A high-end property that comes with state-of-the-art furnishing and services. Such properties have higher prices than standard counterparts.

M

Managed Distribution: A type of service that enables property managers to enhance their online property distribution.

Mark-up: It refers to an increase in price on specific distribution channels.

Merchant of Record: An authorized entity that charges credit cards during bookings.

Minimum Stay: This is the minimum duration required of a guest to reserve before an owner or manager can approve the booking. It comes in handy during on-peak periods where property owners can generate more revenues.

Multi-Calendar: It is a single calendar showing the number of bookings done on all the channels used to distribute listings.

Multi-Family Building: It is a type of apartment or complex in which several long-term renters can occupy. It may also house short-term tenants.

Multi-Unit: A property with several identical units, which can be rooms or apartments.

N

Net Rate: It is the total profit received from a distribution channel after the deduction of commissions.

Noise Monitoring Solution: This is a system that monitors the sound volume on the property and notifies the owner when it exceeds a specified range.

No-Show: It is a situation where a renter or guest who has booked a rental space does not show up or cancel the reservation either.

Non-Refundable Rates: Booking fees of this type comes

at lower rates. However, there are conditions attached. In some cases, guests may have to pay the full booking price even if they cancel or fail to show up during the allocation period. In other words, property owners or managers cannot refund the booking fee.

O

Occupancy: A room or part of a property that is in use or that has been booked.

Occupancy Forecast: It is the process of analyzing a property's occupancy expectation within a timeframe.

Occupancy Rate: This is a process of determining how often a room is being occupied. To achieve this estimation, the total number of booked nights and available nights are added and then divided through with the number of booked nights.

Off-Peak Season: It is the same as the low season.

On Brand: It defines actions taken to showcase a business's brand and message.

Online Payment Service: A web-based platform that helps to process online transactions from a payment card, an e-wallet, or over the internet.

Online Travel Agency (OTA): It refers to a third-party accommodation agent that provides property listings on their online platform. Airbnb, Vrbo, and Booking.com are some of the OTAs available.

Operations: The process of running and maintaining a property or rental business.

OTA Ranking: This involves the use of algorithms to display the position of a listing on a search result page. Factors that influence this ranking include the number and quality of reviews, image quality, reservation click ratio, and response time.

Outdoor Amenities: Exterior features available on a property to improve the guest experience. They could include a basketball court, an outdoor kitchen, or a gazebo.

Outsourcing: It is the act of hiring a third-party to handle specific tasks generally undertaken by in-house persons or entities. An example includes requesting the services of a cleaning company.

Overbooking: A situation where the number of bookings on a property exceeds the availability of rental units.

Over-Improvement: It defines a condition where several unnecessary and non-profiting amenities have been implemented on a property.

Owner's Closet: An off-limit section in a room or property that houses the owner's belongings. Often, this place is usually on lock.

Owners Portal: This is a dedicated dashboard on an accommodation portal through which owners can view specific information on their properties, including their performances.

Owner Revenue: The profit received by a property owner after the manager has deducted the commission due.

P

Payment Gateway: This is an e-commerce system that oversees online transactions (payments) made through various payment methods, including credit cards.

Payment Method: This implies a means by which a person can make payment to another individual or an entity. Credit and debit cards are examples of payment methods.

Payment Processor: It is a system that processes payments. It is also another term for "Payment Gateway."

Payment Scheduling: It involves breaking down the total booking fee into smaller amounts, which are then deducted from a guest's account at specific periods.

Peak Season: Also known as a high season, it is the specific period in a year when travel is at an all-time high. As such, property owners and managers have more bookings.

Pet Fee and Deposit: This is an additional fee that accommodates the lodging of pets and relevant costs attached to it, including cleaning. It is worth noting that such fees are non-refundable. However, deposits are refunded where there is no damage incurred during the guest's stay.

Pet-Friendly: It is a property that accommodates the presence of pets during a stay and provides amenities to cater to them.

Property Management System/Property Management Software (PMS): A system that oversees property management, including reservations and bookings.

Price Per Guest: A pricing allocation that depends on the number of guests lodging in a rental property.

Pricing Structures: It is a pricing system that provides varying rent rates during specific seasons.

Promotions: A discount or bonus offered on a rental property. For example, you could get the third night free when you book during the week.

Property: A short-term or vacation rental apartment.

Property Description: Content that tells visitors what a property is all about and convinces them to make reservations.

Property Manager: A real estate professional hired to oversee rental properties.

Property Management Agreement: A formal document between a property owner and a property manager containing detailed agreements made by both parties, which must be followed to ensure the smooth running of a property.

Property Management Cost: This is the total amount of expenses incurred during property management.

Preparation Time Before Arrival (PTBA): It is the minimum number of days a guest has to book a rental space before arrival. It is also known as "Release Days." As such, managers and owners can prepare for arrivals and also handle last-minute changes effectively.

Q

Qualified Rate: As the name implies, it shows a rate a guest must qualify for to enjoy specific promotions.

Query: It is a request from a potential renter or guest seeking more information on a rental space or listing.

Quiet Hours: These are specific periods during the day which guests are to maintain a minimum volume level on a property.

Quote: A booking price that a property owner or manager offers to potential guests.

R

Rack Rate: An official reservation rate that is negotiable.

Rate Parity: This refers to a legal agreement between an OTA and a property owner, in which both parties agree to the same rates for rental units on all distribution channels, including listing sites.

Real Estate: A property comprising a building(s) and land.

Referred Booking: This is a type of booking made by a guest based on another guest's recommendation.

Refundable Booking: A type of booking or reservation a manager or owner can refund under specific conditions.

Regulations: Guidelines, requirements, and restrictions covering property rentals in a location.

Rental Agreement: A legal document between a property owner and a renter or guest specifying agreements between both parties on specific terms.

Repeat Guests: These are loyal guests that book the same property they lodged in previously.

Reports: A well-documented and comprehensible account of business performance.

Reputation Management: This is a business practice that involves deriving and understanding public opinions on a business and ensuring they are in line with the business goals.

Reservation: It is the act of acquiring rental space for a period. It is another term for "Booking."

Reservation Confirmation: A notification showing a successful booking or reservation.

Reservation Deposit: It is a fee paid to validate a rental contract, which is a percentage of the entire booking cost. For example, a guest can make a reservation for one night's stay for a three-day booking.

Return on Investment (ROI): It is a performance metric that calculates the efficiency of an investment on an asset, such as real estate. Property owners can determine the ROI in rental homes by dividing the property cost by its returns.

Revenue: It defines the entire amount generated within a specific period. Another term for it is "Income."

Revenue Management: It is the use of algorithms to monitor the performance of a rental property over time.

Reviews: They include the opinions and testimonies of previous guests on a property. They help potential guests understand the state of a property, its amenities, and the services provided.

RevPAR (Revenue per Available Room): It is a performance estimation algorithm that calculates the income each available room is supposed to generate. To achieve this result, multiply the average daily room rate (ADR) by its occupancy rate. Another option is to divide the total amount of revenue by the number of available nights.

Room Type: It defines the categorical structure of rental rooms based on size, specifications, and amenities. Each category may come with different pricing.

S

Sales Tax: Depending on the state, with this legal implementation, property owners and managers are to provide the state with lodging taxes on income earned on short-term rentals. It is worth noting that such taxes are paid by the guest.

Scam: It defines a fraudulent scheme perpetrated with the intention to have financial gains from something. In estate, this is becoming an alarming concern. Red flags include the absence of basic language skills, the unavailability of preferred payment methods, unconventional bookings, and strange contact details.

Seasonal Rates: Increased booking fees during high-travel periods, especially in top destinations.

Self-Catering Accommodation: This is a type of property that provides amenities that guests can use to take care of themselves. They could include kitchen facilities.

Self-Check-In: A rental solution that allows guests to

access the property without the intervention of a property owner, manager, or attendant. Often, such accommodation comes with keyless entry systems.

Sell Rate: This is the final booking fee available to guests.

Serviced Apartment: Also known as "Apart-Hotel," this type of property incorporates both an apartment's freedom and privacy and a hotel's facilities in one piece.

Sharing Economy: This refers to a system that is devoid of the traditional peer-to-peer business model.

Single Family House (SFH): A property suitable for a family.

Shoulder Season: It is a travel period between low and high seasons.

Short-Term Rentals: Property guests can rent for a short time.

Smart Home: Accommodation that comes with an integrated system and smart home gadgets that can be remotely controlled.

Smart Locks: A door with an integrated system that can be locked or unlocked remotely (Bluetooth or Wi-Fi) via mobile applications or software.

SNAD (Significantly Not as Described): This term implies that the property bears no similarities to its description on a listing site.

Social Proof: It is a form of evidence that shows other customers or users have, in actuality, bought a product or subscribed to a service, which has provided value. In the rental business, it comes as reviews from previous renters and guests.

Super Host: This Airbnb term describes a host who has provided immense value and guest experience on a large scale.

T

Task Management: This is a system or software that delegates and oversees tasks.

Themed Vacation Rental: This defines a property in which specific rental units or the entire units reflect a theme captivating to guests. As such, they may include themes from popular movies or top destinations. For example, a home can spot a Hawaiian theme for the summer, giving guests a memorable experience.

Third-Party Distribution: Listing sites and companies that display available rental accommodations. They include Airbnb and Vrbo.

Timeshare: An agreement made by several joint owners to convert a home into a holiday apartment using a time-sharing system and an assigned timeframe of one to two weeks per year.

Traveler: A potential guest.

V

Vacation Rental: The process of leasing a furnished property to tourists temporarily. This platform takes out the need to lodge in a hotel.

Vacation Rental Management: A system that enables

property owners and managers to operate and manage a vacation rental business effectively.

Vacation Rental Software: This is a cloud-based system connected to a website, through which guests can book directly, make online payments, access listing sites, and also help property managers to handle reservations and communicate with guests effectively.

Value-Added Items: These are additional features or amenities that enhance guest experience and increase the property's value.

VRMA (Vacation Rental Management Association): This is a group of vacation rental professionals that provide training, connection, and other opportunities to enhance rental businesses.

VRM (Vacation Rental Management) Commission: This is a fee a VRM company charges a rental property owner on the total rental revenue.

W

Weekend Pricing: This pricing structure comes with

varying rates covering Thursdays to Saturdays.

Welcome App: This is a web-based solution or mobile app that enhances a guest experience. Through this application, guests can acquaint themselves with eye-catching services provided by rental business owners and managers, including events, value-added items, and many more.

Welcome Book: It bears similarities to the welcome app. However, this is a physical book guests can use to get comprehensive details on accommodation, including promotions offered.

Welcome Letter: This is a documented material that introduces guests to a rental property. As such, property owners may communicate their heart-warming messages to such individuals even when they are not physically present.

Y

Yield Management: This is a system that considers all aspects of a traveler's behavior to generate a pricing strategy, which can be used to maximize the rental profits on a property.

Chapter 3: An Overview of Airbnb

Having understood the terminology associated with not just Airbnb but real estate as a whole, it is time to check out what this sophisticated and highly rewarding marketplace is all about. One thing that makes Airbnb stand out from the rest is the ability to connect guests and renters with several customized accommodations available within a specified location.

You don't have to go around scouting outing hotel or motel rooms when on tour or a weekend getaway. It is worth mentioning that this online marketplace has spread its tentacles across 191 countries and over 81,000 cities. There are more than 7 million homes available for rent.

In Africa alone, there are more than 1,000 listings available, with enough accommodations to cater to 2 million-plus foreign guests. For guests, this platform has eased property hunting in several ways that were inconspicuous before now. And for the hosts, this is an avenue to generate a sustainable income stream on their properties. It even covers specific risks, such as property damages.

Here are four key points worth stating about the Airbnb solution:

1. Booking an Airbnb is relatively inexpensive compared to a hotel booking.

2. Such an offer is not without its challenges, one of which includes not finding accommodation that meets its description on a listing site.

3. New regulations are in place to accommodate changes in

the Airbnb cancellation policy. I will point out here that these outcomes are based on the occurrence of the novel coronavirus that has ravaged businesses worldwide. Airbnb is flexible enough to handle such unforeseen events to ensure business sustainability.

4. Last but not least, hosts may face severe property damage caused by guests. However, there are mechanisms in place to take care of such unfortunate situations, some of which popped up in the terminology section.

That being discussed, let's cover the advantages and disadvantages of Airbnb, which will help you make your mind on considering this business.

Understanding the Advantages of Airbnb

Vast Range of Homes

One thing you will love about the Airbnb platform, whether you are a host or a guest, is the variety of accommodations that are available and can be provided as well. Ranging from studio apartments to even a castle, this online marketplace has you covered. If you believe your home is worth its value, you can list it and have guests place bookings in their numbers.

Flexibility in Rent Rates

Property owners can set their best available rates or default rates on their property listings. Whereby you have a property you would like to advertise on a listing site, come up with an ideal rate, which can be on a nightly, weekly, or monthly basis.

Free Listings

Who says you have to pay to list your property on the market? With Airbnb, you enjoy free listing. However, to get an ideal response rate from potential guests or travelers, ensure that you use captivating, high-resolution images and eye-catching captions to describe your accommodation.

Custom Searches

Searches on Airbnb are not limited to location and date. You can also look for the desired vacation home via property type, price, value-added items, and even language. To narrow your search further, use specific keywords in the search bar.

Additional Services

Long gone are those days when Airbnb solely centered around property rentals. These days, tourists can search for available restaurants and experiences provided by local Airbnb hosts and super hosts. Interestingly, these listings comprise reviews from hosts and other travelers alike.

Available Protections for Both Parties

Earlier in this segment, I discussed possible challenges guests and hosts may face on Airbnb. Fortunately, a mechanism is in place to cater to both issues. In protecting guests from factors like SNAD and scams, Airbnb retains their payment for 24 hours once they check-in into a rental apartment before releasing the funds to the host.

The hosts are not neglected as there is a guarantee program in place to provide them with insurance of up to $1,000,000. As such, they don't have to worry about covering the cost of repairs on property damaged by the guests. However, this option is available in specific countries.

Understanding the Disadvantages of Airbnb

Discrepancies in Property Descriptions

Back to what I stated before, guests may not get a rental home that matches its description on a listing site. Kindly remember that booking accommodation on this online marketplace bears fewer similarities to making a five-star hotel reservation where you can be assured of getting a rental space as described on the company's website. Property listings are of the property owners; as such, some of them may be more open than others. For this reason, it is essential to check reviews of past guests before booking.

Property Damage

Even though I mentioned a solution in place to handle this problem, it is not available in all Airbnb-domiciled countries. And even if you reside where Airbnb's Host Guarantee Program is present, it doesn't cover everything. For example, you may not be able to recover damaged antique art, destroyed or stolen cash or jewelry, or even injured pets. Besides, the damage deposit, damage protection insurance, or damage waiver fee may not cover the cost of property damaged. Hence, it is essential to conduct guest screening before approving bookings.

Taxes are Unavoidable

For sales tax in the United States, this falls solely on the guests. But that differs from the value-added tax (VAT). If you own an Airbnb property there or in Switzerland, the E.U., or Norway, you have to pay rental income taxes. In the U.S., Form 1042 and Form 1099 are available for hosts to fill their taxpayer details, stating their annual earnings, which Airbnb collects and sends to the Internal Revenue Service (IRS).

Additional Charges

It is worth noting that running an Airbnb business implies that you are subjected to additional fees. However, Airbnb is not the only platform that comes with these costs; hotels and other lodging service providers do the same. First off, guests using this platform pay an additional guest service fee, which may range from 0% to 20%. It helps to cover operational costs, such as Airbnb's customer support. Airbnb shows these fees in the user's currency of choice. Also, processing fees from banks and credit cards may apply when paying through the payment gateway.

Location Restrictions

Unfortunately, not every country supports Airbnb. In specific locations, it is illegal to rent out properties without special permits or licenses. As such, kindly check the local zonal ordinances to find out such qualifications.

The Effect of Covid-19 on Airbnb's Cancellation Policy

Here, I would like to point out that Airbnb has made specific changes to its cancellation policy (an amendment that took effect on March 14, 2020) based on some extenuating circumstances. This action happened three days after the World Health Organization (WHO) declared COVID-19 a global pandemic. Hence, guests who made bookings before the 14th of March and checked-in between the supposed 14th and May 31st could get a full refund.

But that is not all. Airbnb supported hosts affected by this policy with a fund of $250 million. With this strategy, they received 25% of the regular cancellation payment. However, this doesn't apply to bookings done after March 14. Other

Airbnb offers, like Luxury Retreats, Airbnb Luxe, and domestic bookings in countries, like China, which has a $10 million support fund to handle such circumstances.

First Step to Becoming an Airbnb Host

At this point, I believe that I have piqued your interest as you are willing to know what it takes to become an Airbnb host. Before I proceed, let's do a recap of some of the benefits of setting up an Airbnb account:

You can host anytime you want. You are in charge here. Determine when to earn and how to earn.

Set the rates you want. Your nightly prices, pet fees, and deposits, weekend pricing, may vary or hover around that of your competitors.

Create your ideal booking policy, cancellation policy, changeover days, cleaning fee, LOS pricing, and even house rules.

Organize your calendar to handle distributed listings on

multiple channels effectively.

Your listing visibility can reach millions of guests around the world.

The Airbnb community has tons of resources to help you navigate your way through the world of vacation property rentals.

There is a 24/7 customer support that handles inquiries and complaints concerning Airbnb listings.

These are a few benefits you can enjoy being a part of Airbnb. So, what do you need to become a host? Without much further ado, let's set the ball rolling.

It All Begins with the Airbnb Host Page

Visit the Airbnb website (www.airbnb.com) and set up an account. You can sign up using any of the following details: phone number, email address, Apple ID, Google Account, or Facebook Account. Your setup has to be complete before you can list your property.

Choose Your Type of Space

When filling in information on your listing, you will come across several listing types, including a unique space, an apartment, a secondary unit, a house, a boutique hotel, or bed and breakfast.

Select the Kind of Place

Having selected the type (for example, a house), you can move on to the kind of space, which may include a houseboat, a hut, a chalet, a farm stay, a cottage, a bungalow, a cabin, just to mention a few.

Select the Section of the Apartment You'll Be Renting

So, what space on your property are you allocating to your guests? A shared room, a private room, or the entire apartment? Are you setting up the rental space solely dedicated to your guests, or will you be keeping your belongings there as well? Will you be listing Airbnb as part of a company? These are questions you will come across while filling in your listing details.

Complete Other Listing Details

These may include the number of bathrooms, bedrooms, and number of guests you are willing to provide for and accommodate. You need to specify explicitly what will be available, including sleeping arrangements.

Create a Striking, Long-Lasting Impression with Your Listings

Remember, the first impression is everything. What do you expect your potential guests and travelers to see when they come to your listing page? Do you have the right CTA that will drive them towards booking available units? I will cover these aspects in a subsequent chapter, so kindly stay tuned.

Familiarize Yourself with the Local Laws

Don't forget that local laws apply to listing a property on a listing site or an OTA website. For example, NYC (New York City) has stringent rental policies, while cities like London may be lenient. Hence, it is essential to know a city's administrative codes or zoning. In some locations, having a permit or license is a must to operate a vacation rental business.

Pricing is Essential

At this point, familiarize yourself with several rates, including weekend pricing, seasonal rates, and the likes. Determine the price your guests have to pay during high and low seasons. Ideally, set your rates based on a competitive set (Kindly see description under the terminology). Being a start-up, it is recommended that you lower your rates to attract potential guests to your apartment. This was a factor I considered when I listed my property the second time in December 2013, which saw the arrival of my first couple of guests.

As you gain credibility and build the brand reputation, you can catch up to your competitors in terms of pricing. Ideally, start with the price-per-night plan. Also, don't forget to take advantage of Airbnb's Smart Pricing tool. Have your availability calendar and multi-calendar in place to organize bookings.

Consider Other Factors

Have your KPIs, vacation rental software, and property management system (PMS) up and running to manage your vacation rental property, evaluate ROI, and manage the property. Set up pricing structures while considering add-on fees, including cleaning fee and taxes. Your welcome app or book should be on standby to introduce guests to your lodge. By factoring in these elements, your travelers can enjoy an amazing guest experience and become repeat guests over time.

Set Up a Communication Layer

Avoid jumping on the bandwagon of "Instant Booking." I know you want to cut to the chase and have your guests flooding your property in no time. However, it is essential to know who you are dealing with to prevent the problems we discussed earlier on in this book. Additionally, this protection layer gives you more control on which reservations and bookings to approve.

Property owners and managers can get a better understanding of their guests and provide them with the right services when they run through their profiles. How can you tell good guests? Such individuals will communicate with you effectively before their arrival. Also, your response rate and quality matters. Transparency is another element you should not forget in a hurry. For your safety and that of your guests, ensure that all communications revolve within the

Airbnb sphere. Conducting transactions outside this platform may prevent you from enjoying specific protections that may come in handy when a problem arises.

Create a Cancellation Policy

This policy is essential to help you handle impromptu or last-minute cancellations. Your policy can be of any of the following: flexible, moderate, or strict. Having this element in place can help you handle unforeseen circumstances. For example, guests may only have up to 24 hours before a stay to cancel their reservations, after which cancellation becomes impossible. Also, you can set up a non-refundable rate on bookings, which means that if they cancel and you don't have any new booking on that unit or room, you don't record a loss. However, you have to know which one suits your business best. Another way to handle such situations is to have a defined PTBA (Preparation Time Before Arrival).

Outsource Specific Tasks

In reality, you can't solely handle all the tasks concerning property management. From the point of experience, it is ideal to contract some of these jobs to a third-party professional company. For example, you can hire a professional cleaning service to ensure your rental property is neat at all times, giving your guests the best experience. Taking these factors into consideration, you are gradually working your way up to becoming an Airbnb super host.

Become More as An Airbnb Super Host

At this point, nothing stops you from smashing through the roof to attain the designation of a super host in the Airbnb world. You already know how to manage your guests effectively, and your KPIs are pointing in the right direction. Super hosts occupy the top echelons of this online marketplace – you can be a part of them as well. These are individuals with highly reckoned rental services. However, specific factors come into play when gunning for such an enviable position.

Your response rate must be 90% or higher.

You must have secured a minimum of 10 stays per annum.

Your five-star reviews must be 80% or higher. In other words, have an overall rating of 4.8.

Your cancellation rate must be %1 or lower. For example, for every 100 reservations, there should be at most one cancellation. However, there is an exception for those with Airbnb's Extenuating Circumstances policy.

Do these points sound achievable? If you believe it is possible, then it is time to take actionable steps to realize them. It is never too late to start an Airbnb rental business. Build consistency over time, and watch as you gradually rise to become a Super host.

Chapter 4: Airbnb Listing Analysis

Welcome to the world of Airbnb listings, the first step to taking your property public and giving it the view it deserves. I can still vividly picture how elated I felt when I had my first listing – the thrill of knowing that hundreds of thousands of visitors (if not more than a million) could view my apartment. I'm sure you can't wait to hit the send button and launch yours as well. However, one thing you should know is that listing is an essential element in this online marketplace. It can mar or make your vacation rental business, depending on how you go about it. But before that, here are some fun facts on this subject:

1. As of September 30th, 2020, there were 5.6 million active

listings worldwide.

2. Airbnb listings envelope more than 220 countries.

3. There are more than 100,000 cities with Airbnb listings.

How amazing does that sound? But that's not all; Airbnb hosts have generated more than $110 billion in revenue as of October 2020. In actuality, Business Insider has it that Airbnb's listings top those of top five hotel brands combined. Undoubtedly, this is a staggering feat. And you know what? This economic revolution is offering you a chance to become a part of a large community of passive income earners. "But I don't have a complex to offer?" You may complain. Do you have a couch? Do you think you can make an extra buck off it? So, what are you waiting for? However, I like to point out that this business is not for everyone. Why do I state so? The following factors will help you to see my side:

Often, goals are slightly different from expectations. Of course, you want to get your property out there and start making a killing on bookings. However, you have to be realistic about your Airbnb rental goals. First, find out what type of host you intend to become.

Are you comfortable with inviting unfamiliar faces to your home? This is where most people hit the brakes. Guess what? If you are renting a part of your property, then you would have to deal with seeing strange faces daily. However, if that makes you cringe a bit, getting a dedicated apartment solely for this business isn't a bad idea.

Airbnb demands the commitment of resources, like time and effort. You can't avoid that, even if you hire a property manager or use a PMS. Trust me when I say the beginning may not be smooth sailing. However, with the aspects covered in this guide, you should not end up in a maze.

Strategize your listing. I'm going to save this juicy discussion for the next section – Creating a Great Listing on Airbnb. Don't worry, I have you covered.

Work your way around a rented apartment. Of course, how can I forget? Your apartment isn't yours, but you want to host on Airbnb, right? The last thing you want is to get on your landlord's ugly side. I recommend you approach such a person carefully. "But my friends are building theirs successfully without the knowledge of their landlords," you may protest. Here is the thing; nothing buries an Airbnb business faster than an infuriated property owner. And that is the last thing you want. Hence, discuss with your landlord about your intentions and get the individual's views before making a decision. And only do so when you've received clearance.

Your neighbors are not left behind. Chances are you share a property with other individuals. So, you aren't the only one. For this reason, don't go all rampage with Airbnb without notifying them, or else, you may come under fire from angry neighbors who will stop at nothing to see the council place a ban on your Airbnb business. Ensure that they are okay with your idea before you launch.

Starting this business means that you are putting yourself and your property at risk. What happens when you end up permitting a squatter on your property rather than a guest? Who bears responsibility for the damage done to your neighbor's property or vehicle by your guests? What do you do when you wake up one morning to realize that your items are missing? These are factors worth considering before commencing with your vacation rental business.

If you can handle these areas of concern effectively, we can move on to the next segment, which shows you how to create an eye-catching listing on Airbnb.

Creating a Great Listing on Airbnb

As discussed before, setting up an Airbnb account is free – you don't have to pay a penny. However, your success on this platform centers on how you build your rental business. Everyone has a reason for becoming a host on this online marketplace, including me. For some, it is the drive to get an added income stream, while someone else may love to showcase their neighborhood ladened with fascinating events. Regardless of these diverse motives, one thing remains – having a noteworthy listing.

This component is what determines if your potential guests will take action or move on to another offer. The secret to creating a successful listing is to have one that reflects your guests' personalities. What do I mean? It should contain details that give online visitors an amazing guest experience. And this doesn't just entail slapping your property with tons of amenities; you could end up with over improvement. Response rate, politeness, and other minute elements count as well. That being stated, these are some steps worth taking.

Image Quality is a Great Deal!

Have you ever come across some listing pictures that look

like someone had taken them with a 1.3mp sensor camera? Staring at these images for too long may cause you to develop a migraine. No one wants to spend time on listings with such shots, not even me! And here is one of the reasons this type of listing doesn't get the response a property owner thinks it deserves. When potential guests visit a vacation rental listing, they spend more time surfing photos that showcase the look and feel of a listed home. They can imagine what the apartment looks like in reality. Hence, if the image looks shabby, it only sends them scurrying from your page.

Kindly note that having a great listing doesn't only center on image quality but also the appearance of the listed property. A clean rental space attracts more guests than its counterpart. If your images include bedrooms, bathrooms, and other sections of the property, ensure that they are spick and span. As such, guests have an idea of what they are dealing with. Design elements like artworks, flowers, and wallpapers improve the aesthetics of your home. Spice things up by adding a cup of steaming coffee to the view or a white-cover book splashed with bright colors. Check out other competitors' profiles to get a cue or more.

Having completed this step, it is time to take pictures.

Ideally, natural light adds more beauty to a photograph. That is not to state that artificial lights are terrible. Nevertheless, you want to give your audience a feel of your apartment in its natural state. Take shots from several angles of your rental space to reflect depth and style. If your focal point includes your bedroom, add a bed, fluffy pillows, and clean bedding to the scene. Contrastingly, toiletries are not to be revealed in bathroom images; the same goes for dirty dishes in kitchen photos.

Once you have taken these pictures, don't go around splashing them on your profile randomly. The best five photos should sit at the forefront of your listing. These are images of your property's top features. Finally, add riveting captions to them.

Describe Your Property Precisely

Before checking out the listing details of a property, potential guests read through the property description or overview. They want to know what makes your property unique, which will determine if they read further. As a result, it is vital to use words that perfectly describe the appeal, condition, styling, and atmosphere that comes with your rental home. Words like "breath-taking views," "state-of-the-art smart locks," "high-end pristine minimalist furniture," or "floor-to-ceiling double-glazed windows" are words that will draw the attention of your potential guests. Don't also forget to mention the downsides as well, even if they won't be present when they check-in. Remember, transparency is essential in building loyal customers. If you have a hard time coming up with the right words to describe your apartment, have a friend or a colleague do it for you. Their honest opinions go a long way.

Now, it boils down to coming up with a name for your listing. Don't break a sweat. What is your apartment's unique selling points? A top tourist location? A special landmark? Do you have an original painting done by Leonardo Da Vinci or the remains of an 1826 relic? Put it out there. People have to know what makes your property stand out from the rest. If your home is in proximity to a special upcoming event, your guests must know about it. You can provide them with additional services.

Top It Up with a Seven Star Profile

On Airbnb, guests from all walks of life visit several listings to check rental availability of choice. Chances are they will stumble on yours as well. Some of them quickly run through the property owner's profile before studying the accommodation for lease or bookings. A robust profile shows that an Airbnb host is genuine. On the other hand, scanty profiles often depict the owner's personality and, in return, the property's state. I recommend that you use a minimum of 50 words to describe yourself, including areas, like interests and hobbies. Talk about your favorite sport, amazing pet, or even an all-time movie you enjoy. Also, your profile picture should be as stunning as that of your property (high-quality image).

Verification is Paramount

It is not enough to have a profile on Airbnb; you have to verify it to promote trust and transparency. This factor doesn't only help you get credible guests, but it also helps you to verify their identity before approving their reservations or bookings. Moving on from here, another thing worth noting is the use of recommendations on your profile. As a new member of the Airbnb community, you may not have received a booking yet. However, you have to prove to your guests that you can provide a top-notch experience. As such, having recommendations will go a long way. You can achieve this through family members, friends, landlords, past co-occupants, and other individuals you know.

I will let you in on a secret – something I did when I relaunched my Airbnb business that helped secure my guests. Place yourself in the shoes of the travelers and imagine spending one night in your apartment. Detach all familiarities from this rental space and picture yourself coming in for the first time. What is your reaction? Do you like what you see, or are you disappointed? This exercise will give you an idea of what to expect from your guests. Additionally, pay attention to details, regardless of how minute they can be. What a property owner may consider insignificant may pose a great deal to a renter. It is difficult to go wrong with these guidelines in mind.

Airbnb Listing Costs

Airbnb isn't solely for those individuals who are stuck in their home, shuttling between their nine-to-five jobs, and meeting basic house chores or family demands. If you are a frequent holidaymaker, this may be an opportunity to rack up the numbers while scuba diving in the Caribbean. Simply list your apartment on a listing site, like Airbnb, following the details I discussed previously, and voila! You are good to go. However, I must point out that having a strategy can help your rental business succeed, even though this "world" has its complications and setbacks. If you are on your way to becoming a super host, you have to double your efforts to ensure that your business pays off in the end, Big Time! But one question on many would-be hosts is the cost of running Airbnb. Here is my view on this subject.

Operating an Airbnb vacation rental business depends on the type of property you possess or live in (for renters). Also, the amount of time you intend to lease your rental space plays an essential role. Taxes are unavoidable – I have mentioned this at several points.

If the duration of rent per year is 14 days or lesser, this is a short-term rental service that doesn't require you to report your earnings to the IRS. The reason for this is that the revenue service authorities regard such apartments as being personal. But when dealing with Airbnb, watch out for tax forms detailing income statements from hosts. In rare cases, such documents may pop up requesting Airbnb hosts to pay specific undisclosed incomes. For rents under the 14-day timeframe, hosts can send a letter kindly explaining the circumstances of the income and evidence. For this reason, it is vital to keep track of all earnings for future events.

What if the Airbnb property isn't your primary residence? For vacation homes and other related properties, you have to report your income generated via rental. This is filed under Schedule E. Deduct all rental costs, separating them from expenses (for example, utility bills) incurred during personal use. You have to consider the following expenditures – supplies, service fees, insurance, and maintenance.

Starting with the first in line, you have to keep your guests comfortable at all times. The provision of clean towels, bedding, and adequate amenities is a must. You may have to get security compartments to house some valued items or keep specific things out of bounds. All these items will set you back several bucks. So, it is essential to consider this when determining operational costs.

Service fees are non-negotiable, regardless of the type of cancellation policy set by the host. You can't dodge them. For your payment process, expect to pay Airbnb 3% in commissions. It is worth noting that this includes additional guest, pet charges, and cleaning fees. Special Airbnb hosts with stringent cancellation policies (Super Strict 60 days) pay 5% as service fees. On the other hand, guests pay way more, ranging from 12% to 15%.

Insurance policies are great. However, you have to know what you are signing up for before committing your resources. Some coverages apply to short-term rentals. However, if they are frequent, you may have to get a policy that covers a bed and breakfast or a hotel. A rental dwelling policy may come in handy for longer rentals. This type of insurance is 25% higher than the traditional homeowner's policy. Another alternative is to get a landlord. You have to take cognizance of these costs when running an Airbnb. Insurance policies are there to protect you from specific, unfortunate outcomes.

As an Airbnb host, your rental space must be clean. Often, you may not have the time to get this done due to other pressing demands. Hiring a professional cleaning service may save you time, money, and effort in the long run. But kindly bear in mind that this is not free. Cleaning fees will apply. Nonetheless, you can strike a good bargain with a reputable cleaning service provider.

Considering these factors, you can decide if Airbnb is worth your time and effort. It doesn't guarantee overnight success – in actuality, nothing does. On the brighter side, you can generate a sustainable income.

Chapter 5: Types of Property Available For Airbnb

When signing up on Airbnb, you have a vast list of property types to choose from. However, this has not always been the case. Let's take a trip down memory lane; approximately 13 years ago, this robust online rental marketplace had only three airbeds – courtesy, Brian Chesky and Joe Gebbia, the notable Airbnb co-founders. They provided travelers with rental opportunities from their San Francisco apartment, which has grown to become a household name in the real estate world.

Currently, there are about 4.5 million accommodation spaces in 81,000 cities worldwide. Hosts on this platform have generated income surpassing a whopping $41 billion, with an occupancy rate exceeding 300 million. Isn't that mind-boggling? But that is the tip of the iceberg; Airbnb expanded their property types to accommodate new ones. They include:

Vacation Home

Unique

B&B

Boutique

Airbnb has added these new properties to the existing ones – Entire Home, Private Room, and Shared Space. But that is not all to the improvement made; there are new tiers as well. They include:

Airbnb Plus

Additionally, I will discuss the Airbnb Collection entry that makes it possible for travelers and other individuals to find the perfect home for any occasion. And the last part worth mentioning is the revamped Super host program, coupled with the "Guest Membership" program that Airbnb included a couple of years back. With these features, Airbnb has transcended the accommodation rental business. Here is what Brian Chesky has to say about the remodeled Airbnb online platform:

10 years ago, we never dreamed of what Airbnb could become. In fact, people thought the idea that strangers would stay in each other's homes was crazy. Today, millions of people every night do just that. But we want to go further by supporting and expanding our community so that in 10 years' time, more than 1 billion people per year will experience the benefits of magical travel on Airbnb.

7 Available Property Types

In summary, there are seven property types: Vacation Home, Unique, B&B, Boutique, Entire Home, Private Room, and Shared Space. So, let's talk about the types of Airbnb rentals.

You may have spent more time than average on the Airbnb platform and already know your way around. However, if that is not the case, you have to understand some subtle details that encapsulate this online marketplace. There are some factors renters look out for when checking out an apartment.

Entire Home

What does this term mean? You may ask. When an Airbnb home is up for rent or booking, a guest or traveler may have the option to select "Entire Place." What this means is that they have the entire rental space to themselves. No other guests or travelers share a section of the property or use specific amenities, like the bathrooms or kitchen. In other words, there is full privacy. That is not to state that renters can share outdoor facilities (BBQ, garden, or a swimming pool) with others – that option is available, depending on what you want. However, amenities and rental spaces are meant to offer guests exclusivity.

Private Room

Let us assume that your home comprises five bedrooms and you are willing to rent one of them out to a guest; Airbnb provides this option. All you have to do is to specify the number of available units available for rent. Remember that this option works effectively when there are house rules in place. You may decide not to share specific indoor amenities, such as your kitchen. How about bathrooms? Of course, your Airbnb guests need a place to freshen up now and then. But if they are sharing such amenities, it is ideal to specify how many individuals are entitled to them.

Unique Stays

Not everyone wants to rent a studio apartment or a condo in the city. Some individuals are looking for unique rental spaces, like a cabin beside a lake, in the countryside, or a yurt in the woods. If you have such spaces for rent, do not hesitate to list them on the Airbnb platform.

Shared Space

It is worth noting that some travelers out there don't have the money to splurge on a single rental unit, and as such, need a rental space within their tight budget. Such individuals fall within the younger age group, for example, college students. Airbnb hosts with rooms featuring more than one bed can put the unit up on the platform's listing site. What this means is that such guests can share a room, which is a win-win for them and you as well.

Vacation Home

As the name implies, this apartment is your second residence, which you can list on Airbnb. Travelers and guests can occupy this home when you are away. So, why have an unoccupied secondary condo in LA when you can use it to make more money? Airbnb provides you with such a lucrative option.

B&B

At this point, I see eyebrows being raised. "Isn't Airbnb the same as B&B?" You may ask out of curiosity. Not all hosts may know that there is a difference. For the sake of clarity, I will discuss this aspect in a jiffy. Airbnb provides hosts and guests with a home-sharing network. On the other hand, B&B centers around the traditional bed and breakfast. But don't worry; I get it – you may still have a hard time keeping up with my definition. Hence, I will delve further into this topic. First off, here is what Heather Turner, who is the marketing director of the Professional Association of Innkeepers International (PAII), has to say about the B&B

platform:

Airbnb has co-opted the B&B name. The terms, Airbnb and B&B, are used interchangeably by guests and journalists."

Although Airbnb and B&B may look alike, the former comprises a home-sharing site with less-stringent regulations, while the latter is an inn backed by local or state lodging regulations. You can liken this to a mini-hotel with additional personalized features. Interestingly, the Airbnb platform encapsulates B&B services. As such, you can run the traditional bed and breakfast business model on Airbnb. Some individuals even run their rental businesses on the listing site like B&Bs, especially those in parts of Scotland, Amsterdam, Ireland, just to mention a few.

Now, this is where it gets unique; the B&B stands out as the last letter is more pronounced. Such lodging services come with a complimentary full breakfast. How about that? Does that sound like something you would love to offer your guests? I presume the same. There is no limit to what you can serve, including pastries, yogurt, cereal, and fruits. Often, the B&B owner resides on a property close to the rental space to ensure satisfaction for the guests.

Boutique Hotels

Okay, this term may sound strange to you if you are a newbie on the Airbnb platform. But I will break it down to aid comprehension. What is a boutique hotel or a boutique home? This 80s or 90s-styled mini-hotel comprises 10 to 100 rooms. Such apartments feature unique selling points and unique settings that are scalable.

So, that's it for the property type. Now, let's talk about Airbnb collections. Do you know that the initial business model of this robust rental platform catered solely to solo travel? Yes, it did. However, as time progressed, additional travel options came into the scene. With Airbnb collections, you can find the ideal home that meets your travel needs; whether you intend to camp in the woods on a family vacation or you want an apartment with extra amenities and rooms for rent, the online marketplace has you covered.

Airbnb Tiers

Also, speaking of tiers, there is the "Airbnb Plus" and the "Beyond by Airbnb."

Airbnb Plus

The Airbnb community is thinking in line with luxury and comfort. As such, they have added a new rental tier that meets such a benchmark. Such apartments come with personal verification before being listed on the site. Initially, there were 2,000 units of this tier in more than ten cities (13 to be factual). Now, the number has increased. So, how does an apartment meet this standard? There is a 100+ point checklist. This rating parameter spans design, comfort, and cleanliness. Homes that meet this evaluation gets top placement, alongside the following:

Professional photography

Design consultation

Premium support

Beyond by Airbnb

Most travelers imagine enjoying a trip of a lifetime, where they get to enjoy nothing but the best. As such, Airbnb luxury has come to stay, providing world-class guest experience in the world's finest homes.

Investing in a Property

Airbnb isn't solely for those individuals who are stuck in their home, shuttling between their nine-to-five jobs, and meeting basic house chores or family demands. If you are a frequent holidaymaker, this may be an opportunity to rack up the numbers. If you have a property of interest – one, which you can finance either partially or entirely, you can take the next investment step. And even if you don't have the money, this section is still relevant to your real estate investment. The first step to take is to find the ideal property that will generate the right rental cash flow. Additionally, this is where your Airbnb hosting journey begins. For some individuals, hiring a certified Airbnb property manager may be a step in the right direction. So, how can you invest in a property for your Airbnb rental business?

Pinpoint the Ideal Cities that Promote Airbnb

I believe that location is everything in the world of real estate. This factor determines your success or setbacks in an Airbnb business. In this regard, you have to consider a property in a location that supports short-term rental profitability. But how can you say that a city is Airbnb-friendly? Kindly examine the laws and regulations of this rental business. It is no news that specific top tourist spots have cracked down on Airbnb property owners that provide short-term leases, with some places implementing a complete ban. Another area that has come under the same stringent policy is a non-owner occupied rental.

What does this mean? Investors cannot purchase an investment property to rent the entire unit. As such, those owners that are resident on-site can venture into the rental business. Locations that promote this policy include Las Vegas and Los Angeles. If you are looking for Airbnb-friendly cities in the U.S., the following places should be on your list:

Cleveland, OH	Gatlinburg, TN	Milwaukee, WI	Tempe, AZ
Phoenix, AZ	San Antonio, TX	Tampa, FL	Indianapolis, IN
El Paso, TX	Kissimmee, FL	Memphis, TN	Columbus, OH
Kissimmee, FL	Philadelphia, PA	Houston, TX	Fort Lauderdale, FL
Atlanta, GA	Dallas, TX	Mesa, AZ	

These are locations where you can invest in an Airbnb property. If you have found one that aligns with the above-discussed policy, you can start considering other aspects, like zoning laws, Airbnb taxes, licenses and permits, Airbnb occupancy limits, rental property codes, potential tourism forecast, and statistics. I presume you need a property that can fetch you a high monthly rental income, but you have no idea how to identify one. There is no need to fret as there are specific parameters to look out for, especially with the housing market:

The first thing you will notice about the housing market is its high average Airbnb daily rate.

The above-mentioned parameter tends to indicate a high average monthly Airbnb rental income.

That being stated, let us look at its "Occupancy Rate." Kindly bear in mind that your focus should not be solely on the rental charge and income generation. Depending on the city you reside in, you have to consider your property occupancy rate, which stems from the average rate of your location. Some property owners may earn decent cash flow, having a low Airbnb occupancy rate and a high average daily rate. Ideally, there should be a balance. Also, note that no location provides a 100% occupancy rate. Focusing on this expectation can be likened to expecting a pot of gold at the end of the rainbow.

Nevertheless, you can get a property with a significant potential ROI. In that case, another area worth considering is the cap rate, preferably anywhere between 8% and 12%. Interestingly, it is easy to find stats on Airbnb tourism and laws using the Google search engine. On the other hand, you may need special software to find the following "by City":

Airbnb rental income

Airbnb daily rates

Airbnb cap rates

Airbnb occupancy rates

Mashvisor's investment property blog provides free information on these areas. You can find an ideal Airbnb home to invest in by viewing the real estate industry through the eyes of a realtor and an Airbnb guest. Hey, it's 2021 and guess what? The real estate market is changing significantly – thanks to several factors, including the COVID-19 pandemic. Hence, you may want to include in your search the following:

Top profitable Airbnb locations worth investing in 2021

Top places to purchase a vacation home in 2021

Of course, such keywords will narrow your search and help you find a vast list of ideal properties that are up for sale.

Locate a Top Airbnb Neighborhood in Your Selected City

Here, we are using the top-to-bottom approach to locate the best Airbnb property. Once you have found the best Airbnb-friendly city (for example, San Antonio, Texas), it is time to find which part offers the best deal for your rental business; this requires you to conduct an analysis. For this, you need a heatmap analysis tool. What does it mean? It is a system that helps you locate the best location for your Airbnb business based on the following criteria:

Occupancy rate

Listing price

Cash on cash return

Rental income

Mashvisor provides a heatmap tool to aid you in your search.

Compare Properties to Get the Best Deal

Now, you have found some properties that meet your requirement and that of the business. So, 80% of your work is complete, the remaining part entails comparing Airbnbs to get the best deal. With Mashvisor's rental property finder, you can find top homes with a significant cap rate. But how do you do that? It's simple; use filters, like rental strategy, budget, distance (from the city), property type, number of bathrooms and bedrooms, and other amenities. This time, you are closer to finding the ideal property for your Airbnb investment.

Investment Analysis Comes into Play

Once you have completed the steps discussed above, it is time to analyze your Airbnb options critically. Finding properties that match your heatmap search doesn't imply that you whip out your purse or wallet immediately to make a down payment. You still have to be sure about your rental business profit generation. And this is easier with a profit calculator. As usual, Mashvisor provides you with one, which combines data from reliable sources, like Airbnb and MLS. You can look at the verified property listing performance of Airbnb hosts within a timeframe.

This evaluation doesn't take a toll on your time. Find a high-performing rental vacation home based on cash flow, estimated costs, rental income, cap rate, occupancy rate, cash on cash return, just to mention a few. And yes, you may have a unique financing option (either cash payment or a mortgage plan). For this, you need an integrated mortgage calculator. If you are not financing the property with your money (mortgage), you need to provide the following:

Loan term

Mortgage type

Down payment

Interest rate

Comparative Market Analysis (CMA) is of Utmost Priority

So, you have found the best rental property; what amount can you afford? At this point, you need a realtor's help. However, you can also conduct a CMA to find the value of the investment home. This analysis uses specific metrics of similar properties within the home's location, including listing prices. With this, you can get a home at a competitive price. Your real estate agent will also help you get in touch with the property owner to strike a deal.

Optimizing the "Rental Arbitrage" Platform

You may have heard the term "rental arbitrage." But what does it mean? Let's start by defining the word arbitrage; that will give you an idea of what we are dealing with in this section. When you buy an item at a low price and sell it at a high price for profit, such an act is known as arbitrage. So, if you rent a home for $1,800 per month and sublet it on a listing platform for $3,100, you are running "rental arbitrage." Your expenses for each month may hover around $300 (including Airbnb charges). Your net profit is $1,000.

"Is this rental option legal?" you may ask. I will state that it depends on your area of residence. You have to find a location that supports rental arbitrage. But it doesn't end there; discuss with your landlord about this platform. Once cleared, ensure to have the agreement legally documented with the inclusion of Airbnb's host protection insurance. What are the steps to take with this rental option?

It is worth noting that not all cities provide Airbnb investors and hosts with rental arbitrage, especially when short-term rentals come into play. As such, it is essential to research the Airbnb market in this regard. The Airbnb website is your go-to platform for this market analysis. You have to consider:

Proximity

Property type

Property design

Number of bathrooms and bedrooms

Amenities

Attraction centers within the property location, including parks, shopping centers, clubs, and the likes.

One way to get such information is to look out for online reviews on listing sites and check out what reputable travel blogs are saying about the real estate market in your location. You also have to check out the potential ROI of properties within such a neighborhood, including the use of average rental rates and occupancy rates. Remember, you will be comparing Airbnb homes to help you set your rental price accordingly while factoring in the weekend and nightly rates.

Bear in mind that the former tends to be higher than the latter, depending on activities within your location. The difference between both rates will determine the average daily rental rate. Peak and off-peak seasons are factors that influence your rental cash flow. Don't forget to include maintenance costs when calculating your potential Airbnb monthly income. An Airbnb profit calculator should help you identify the above-discussed elements.

Look at the Financial Implications for Your Start-up

In actuality, what is worth doing at all is worth doing well. The last thing you want is to venture into a business that you can't see to the end. As such, one of the areas to identify when starting an Airbnb is the cost. How much do you have to start? You may not have a home like I did when I started my Airbnb journey in 2013. So, here are some expenses worth noting:

Deposit

Application fee, including credit history evaluation and background check

Furnishing

LLC filing (if needed)

Move-in fee

Legal fees

And even when you have all these costs in place, don't expect to break even overnight. Sometimes, it takes weeks, months, or a little over a year to realize your profit. But when you do, it becomes possible to analyze your potential Airbnb monthly cash flow.

Property Listing

At this point, you have to showcase your property to potential travelers and guests. This phase is straightforward, especially on the Airbnb listing platform. The website has a tab signifying the "Become a host" option. Select it and follow the instructions. To understand how property listings work, you can create a dummy profile to check out some elements of the site. Once ready, create rental parameters, including nightly prices, available nights, requirements, and many more. Ensure that you build an attractive profile that will capture the eyes and minds of your potential guests.

Business Optimization

Your rental business has commenced. Now, it is time to improve your rank on the listing site to attract more guests. Here is where most Airbnb hosts get stuck – a similar experience I had some months after I launched my Airbnb business. One of the reasons these individuals hit a brick wall is the poor listing photography. In truth, the closest online visitors are to seeing and feeling your property is through photos. As such, it is essential to have high-resolution images of your Airbnb home listed on the platform. Not everyone can capture great photographs. For this reason, a professional photographer's services come in handy.

But is there all there is to Airbnb profile optimization? Of course, not. When describing your rental home, use the right keywords. Some tools aid popular searches using this strategy. You can also filter your search by identifying the keywords of highly-rated Airbnb accommodations in the real estate industry. Find out how these property owners display sections of their rental units, including living rooms, bedrooms, bathrooms, and kitchens.

Business Automation

Perhaps, you have optimized your Airbnb profile; it is time to automate it. You don't have to work round the clock to run a successful Airbnb or multiple Airbnbs – this is time-consuming and energy-draining. If you want to be a successful host or a potential super host. It is essential to have ideal automation systems in place to ensure that your rental business runs smoothly. They may include yield management, vacation rental management, task management, self-check-in, and property management system. You can also have a property manager or co-host that will help you oversee the business. Interestingly, Airbnb oversees the booking technicalities; so, you don't have to worry about processing guests' reservations.

Let's talk about hiring a co-host. Over time, your rental business may exceed your capacity, that you have no other option but to get an extra hand to oversee its affairs. But not everyone qualifies to run your Airbnb, regardless of your relationship with them. Certainly, you need a trustworthy person, but that is not enough. Such an individual must understand the real estate market and be hospitable enough to provide top-notch guest experiences. This person will be your Airbnb rental representative – one whom your guests will deal with directly. Is it possible to have multiple co-hosts? Yes, it is, especially if you have several property listings. As time progresses, there may be a need for an asset manager.

How about your property check-in process? That is one area you can't ignore if you want to give your Airbnb guests the best experience. Why should you have to come around all the time to show them to their rooms when you could integrate sophisticated smart locks into your home or use the traditional lockbox? They can even access their rental units remotely from their smartphones. And if you are concerned about welcoming such guests to your property, you can prepare a detailed welcome app, book, or letter that will show them the following:

Wi-Fi passwords

Available amenities

Transportation means

Gate codes

Top attraction sites

Emergency contacts

Co-host contact details, and many more.

As such, your guests don't have to barrage your phone lines with calls as they have almost all the details they need. Is there anything else worth noting? In reality, you don't need an investment property to become an Airbnb host. There are several options out there, including using your garage, spare bedroom, or even your recreational vehicle (RV). This strategy will help you to generate monthly cash flow.

How to Minimize Costs and Maximize Your Profits

I presume that you have come across stories of Airbnb hosts and super hosts making thousands of dollars annually, including mine. But here is something you should know – not all Airbnb businesses turn out to be profitable. But here is what makes a successful rental business – hard work and smart work.

I have put in years of experience to sustain my Airbnb as a super host, taking into account my first year of failure as a host. Here is what I have to say; Airbnb is one heck of a ride – one, which you will find interesting as you progress. From a successful landlord's perspective, here are some things to consider when running your rental business:

Consistent Property Listing Updates

Kindly note that Airbnb is not the same as Amazon or eBay. It is not a general advertising site; rather, it is a "smart" listing site that gives online visitors an ideal, customized rental apartment based on specific parameters. I will clearly state that there is no room for vacancies, considering the fact that you are taking this as an additional source of income. It is not enough to have your profile in place; you must ensure that it stays up to date, even when you've already uploaded eye-catching photos and generated tons of positive reviews. Your property description must stay "alive." On Airbnb's part, there are constant updates available to better the Airbnb community and provide both hosts and guests with the best experience. For this reason, you have to keep abreast of such changes.

Long-Term Hosting

Do you need a significant monthly cash flow? Then, you have to think long-term. What do I mean by this statement? Making preparations for guests' arrivals can be time-consuming and financially demanding. Even though they pay for cleaning costs, you may have to spend additional expenses on maintenance to keep your rental property attractive. Such expenditure tends to skyrocket when there are multiple short-term bookings on rental units, leaving the owner with little profit. But does that mean that short-term rentals are bad? Definitely, not; on-site hosts will find this niche extremely profitable. However, if you consider your time to be a valuable element and desire to earn substantial income from your rental business, long-term hosting is the way to go.

Potential Rental Generation for Long-Term Rental

One of the things you will notice about the real estate rental industry is its dynamism. More people gravitate towards renting properties than owning one. Hence, long-term rentals seem to be the order of the day, especially for millennials and baby boomers. For property owners that are into short-term rentals, it is essential to look out for long-term profitability if they want a sustainable Airbnb business. Find out what the long-term real estate market is saying in comparison to your net income. There may be a need to adjust nightly rates and other rental parameters to ensure business longevity; this is where a pricing calculator comes into play. Factor in location and occupancy rate.

With the above-listed strategies, you can't go wrong with your Airbnb business. In case you missed out on some parts discussed in this section, here is a summary of what you should do to minimize costs and maximize your profit:

Keep your property listing constantly updated

Target long-term hosting

Check out the potential profit generation of long-term rentals

When you consider these factors, it becomes easy to run your Airbnb rental business.

Chapter 6: Airbnb Legalities

Hopefully, with the sections you have covered so far, you've been able to gather in-depth information on how to start and run a successful Airbnb business. But there is still more. At this point, you have to know how to handle the legal aspect of this business. Trust me, you may come across some controversies over time. Nevertheless, Airbnb's success amid several challenges is hinged on two things:

1. Property owners and renters searching for an additional

income source, and

2. Travelers looking for cheaper alternatives to hotels.

No doubt, many hosts make a killing in the Airbnb rental industry; however, this success does not come on a platter of gold. Before starting this business, you have to put several elements into perspective.

Legal Options to Consider

Becoming an Airbnb host is no walk in the park; you may come across some legal risks while running your Airbnb. Hence, you have to take your rental business seriously to ensure that it is within the confines of the city, state, and federal codes and laws. So, where do we begin?

Understanding City Laws

It is not enough to find a city that is Airbnb-friendly; you also have to know its code and regulations concerning rentals. Does your property align with its zoning laws? Is it within its allowable limits? What duration is required for subletting? Not all cities have the same requirements, which can be mind-boggling for a newbie. However, understanding such regulations will help you run a successful rental vacation home business without facing steep fines, especially in cities like San Francisco and New York. So, research thoroughly on what your city demands of your rental business before commencing.

Find Out if Your City Allows Subletting

If the property you reside on isn't your own, you have to communicate with your homeowner association (HOA) or other related organizations on the issue of subletting. You may find your colleagues leasing their homes to guests without cross-checking their lease agreement on this subject. Like I stated before, being in your landlord's bad books can be catastrophic. Such individuals may not hesitate to facilitate an eviction on such grounds. Not all property owners will buy the idea of subletting their homes to Airbnb guests. For this reason, you have to dot your I's and cross your T's to be on the safer side. Get documented permission from your landlord and homeowner association before embarking on this course.

Get a License

Running an unregistered Airbnb can cost so much in fines —

and I am sure that you wouldn't want such to happen. If you intend to run a short-term rental, kindly obtain a permit. Currently, some cities have imposed stringent regulations to weed out illegal Airbnb businesses, including San Francisco and Boston. It is not uncommon to find large commercial establishments manipulating the rental industry for profit-making while posing as Airbnb enterprises. To avoid falling on the wrong side of the law, make sure that you obtain a permit to host your Airbnb home.

Taxes are Essential

I have mentioned the issue of taxes in several parts of this guide. In truth, you cannot avoid this element. Several Airbnb hosts have enjoyed user privacy on the robust online marketplace as the platform keeps their data private. But on the other hand, some of them have evaded taxes based on this condition. In return, some cities have enforced stringent regulations to combat this act. I understand that there are several needs to address now and then; nevertheless, some things are not worth avoiding, not even taxes.

And if it gets extremely tough, Airbnb may be forced to release such information, which may affect hosts that fail to comply in this aspect. The last thing you want is to receive a hefty fine with accumulated taxes. Unfortunately, Airbnb will not be there to save the day. It is your responsibility to pay taxes.

Have an Insurance Policy in Place

When running Airbnb, you will come across different guests from all walks of life. Sometimes, such individuals may pass guest screening and still cause chaos on your property – I have experienced this more than twice. In such a situation, a robust insurance plan will save you time, money, and effort. Of course, no property owner wants damage to their rental vacation homes, but as they say, "stuff happens." Such a disaster may not be within the confines of a regular homeowner's plan.

"But Airbnb provides insurance coverage of up to $1 million..." you may say. And that is true. But check the fine print – it doesn't cover everything. There are some exclusions. Do not overrule the chance of such events happening; this is a regrettable action to take. To safeguard your property, have an insurance policy in place.

Don't Overlook the Place of Health and Safety

At the moment, one of the factors that differentiate hotels, motels, and other standard hospitality industries from Airbnb rentals is health and safety. However, don't overlook the fact that injuries are bound to occur on your premises, some of which may result in legal consequences, especially when the property's health and safety measures are questionable. You may want to check Airbnb's guidelines in this regard. Your rental vacation home must have some basic items, including the following:

A fire extinguisher

A first-aid kit

Functional carbon monoxide detectors

Smoke alarm

Listed emergency contacts

Proper ventilation systems

Highlighted fire escape route

The building wiring should be intact and out of sight to prevent electrical hazards. The heaters and air conditioners should be fully operational to keep guests comfortable. In promoting health and safety, set occupancy limits. Additionally, here is something I want to point out concerning this aspect. Having such limits in place will also keep guests safe during this COVID-19 pandemic. As a plus, you can station face masks and other PPEs at strategic points of the property. Understand that such actions may cut into your cash flow, but over time, it sets your rental business on the path to becoming extremely successful and saves you from legal issues.

Overseeing Tax Issues and Other Legal Matters

In the previous section, I listed tax as one of the factors to consider when operating Airbnb rental services. But there is more to what I discussed there, which we will be looking at shortly. But let me start by stating that you don't need an entire property to get started – I'm sure you've heard this several times. A room is enough to begin the journey. And as you earn, you also spend, including state and federal income tax. This subject is intricate. So, let's breakdown this subject into several parts:

Short-Term Rental Taxation – Less Than 14 Days Per Year

If you have a rental vacation home that you lease less than 14 days per year, you won't have to pay tax on your rental income, regardless of the amount earned. Yes, that is right – you 'clearly' read that part. So, even if you make $3,000 during such periods, the IRS can be unaware of such earnings – no harm, no foul play. Also, if the duration personally spent on your home exceeds 14 days or 10% of the total rental days (at a fair rental price), you don't have to report your income to the IRS, according to IRC Sec. 280A(g). it is easy to meet the personal use requirement if you reside in the home used for Airbnb rental. But if this is not the case, it becomes essential to monitor your non-rental days. Under this eligibility, you don't have to do the following:

Factor in the depreciation deduction

Deduct operating expenses

File Schedule E (This is a form that contains details of rental income and expenses)

Why don't you have to do any of these? The answer is simple; according to the IRS, your home doesn't fall under the rental property classification. But what happens when such a property lease exceeds 14 days? Let's find out about that in the next section.

Rental Taxation Exceeding 14 Days Per Year

You may have an apartment that you rent for more than 14 days a year or one that you live in for more than such duration; you don't enjoy a tax-free rental income. Oops, that sounds discouraging, right? But hey! We pay taxes on almost everything – it is what it is. You have to report whatever you earn during this period to the IRS. You will file the IRS Schedule E and tax return after deducting rental expenses. As a property owner under this classification, you cannot avoid income tax as well; this comes from your net profit. Kindly note that your rental income determines your annual deductions.

So, what do you do when your rental income is less than your expenses? In such a situation, you don't have to balance up from other income sources; rather, the loss extends to future earnings, which is deducted from such incomes. Understand that there are limitations to such deductions. Such stringent policies are in place to prevent property owners from deducting personal expenses in place of rental expenses. So, let us discuss some of the expenses for clarification's sake.

General Expenses

The first area you may want to look at when addressing such deductions is your general expenses. They include:

Maintenance fee (cleaning, internet connection, gardening, and many more)

Home insurance

Real estate taxes

Mortgage interests

Repairs

When factoring in such expenses, ensure that they are within the rental duration. Deduct such period from the entire duration of use. What do I mean? Let's assume that you live on your property for 215 days and rent it out for 150 days. The rental duration in percentage is 41%. Hence, you have to deduct this figure from your general expenses, which are, in turn, deducted from your rental income. Another approach to this deduction is to deduct a part of your rental unit expenses from that of your entire property. For example, if you have a three-room apartment and rent one of them, you could deduct 1/3 of your general expenses.

Direct Rental Expenses

Unlike the first expense discussed above, you can deduct your entire direct rental expenses. But what are they? You may ask. These are expenses regarding:

Credit checks

Rental fees and commissions

Rental insurance

Advertising

Rental repairs

Depreciation

Cleaning costs

Pass-Through Deduction

Based on the Tax Cuts and Jobs Act (TCJA) introduced on November 2, 2017, short-term rental businesses can benefit from this deduction. With this implementation, property owners under this category can deduct up to 20% of their rental income from their income taxes. But what happens when the taxable income exceeds specific points? The IRS will have to consider deductions based on:

50% of the W2 wages

25% of wages in addition to 2.5% of the cost of depreciable business property

It is worth noting that a business can encapsulate a short-term rental activity, which, in turn, qualifies as a pass-through. What does this mean? Individuals, partnerships, LLCs, or, in some rare cases, S corps, own and operate such businesses. So, Airbnb hosts that provide such services can take advantage of this option.

Legal Issues Concerning Bed and Breakfast/Hotel Services

For tax purposes, renting out a portion of your property is no different from operating a hotel or a bed and breakfast business. It becomes more established under such services when you have dedicated rooms that you don't live in that generate rental income. If your Airbnb services are customer-centric (room cleaning services), you could as well be running a hotel business. As such, such rental services fall under the business category. What this means is that your rental income comes with:

Self-employment taxes – Medicare and Social Security

Such tax implications may put a financial strain on Airbnb hosts' incomes. However, there are no restrictions on deductions. Deducting annual losses generated may still come with specific limits. How do you report your expenses and income? This time around, you will file the IRS Schedule C or Form 1040. Is there a way to prevent this business classification? Yes, there is. You don't have to offer substantial customer-centric services to your guests. In other words, avoid providing them with cleaning services, laundry services, and breakfasts. A cleaning fee should be in place aside from the rental fee, which Airbnb guests pay when checking out of a rental property.

Handling Positive and Negative Reviews Effectively

Having a bad review on Airbnb can be nightmarish for any host. However, you don't have to beat yourself up and throw in the towel. Such reviews can go in your favor if you know what to do. I would like to mention that potential Airbnb guests look out for negative reviews when checking out listing properties. Such feedback helps them have a bird's eye view of a property owner's or property manager's services in relation to the guest's experience. However, if there are tons of negative opinions about a rental business, such a host may lose bookings. No one wants to have such an encounter. But you know what? Not everyone will be optimally satisfied with a service. The term "guest experience" is relative, such that it differs from one person to another. Even as an Airbnb host, I still deal with customers' complaints – it is part of staying in business. Nevertheless, I create a winning strategy for them.

Most Airbnb hosts think that negative reviews signify the end of a rental business. That is far from reality. They serve as performance-checking mechanisms. They are there to keep your business in shape. So, how do you handle such reviews and turn them into your business' strong points? Let's identify these strategies. But before we proceed, I will state that you should maintain professionalism when dealing with either a positive or negative review. That being out of the way, it is time to commence.

Request a Change in Rating

The easiest and most straightforward way to revise a negative rating is to have the guest change it to a positive one. But don't expect to happen at the wave of a magic wand, especially if such an individual had an awful experience on your rental property. You have to sincerely apologize to this person and promise to make up for such an experience, either by providing a partial refund or any other means, in exchange for a fair rating. You have to be careful about your response and request. Even if the review stays the same, the rating can help your business to maintain a good record with Airbnb.

Remove Negative Reviews with Airbnb's Help

Let me state here that not all reviews are genuine. Some are intended to purposely hurt one's business. I have had such an encounter before and used it to my advantage. So, let me show you how to go about it. You may come across a negative review that violates Airbnb's Content Policy. In such a situation, kindly get in touch with the company to have it removed. But this is not as simple as "speaking with the manager." It is imperative that you provide them with a strong case. Airbnb can remove negative reviews if they include:

Extortion

Spam

Incentivized opinions, and

False experiences

On your end, you have to ensure that your services do not contravene Airbnb terms and conditions. All communications are to be within the online listing platform.

By doing so, the company will not find you wanting when they review your request.

Delay Reviews

According to Airbnb, there is a 14-day window for guests to post their reviews on the platform. However, Airbnb hosts can delay this option for a specific period. If, by any chance, your guest has a bad experience, implementing this strategy can give them enough time to cool down, after which they can leave a less-damaging review on your listing. But there is more. Airbnb will not prompt your guest to leave feedback as well, since you have submitted yours.

Respond to Reviews

We all love to get a response when we have complaints on specific issues, and this is no different from Airbnb guests. One of the ways to tell a reputable host from the rest is to check out how they handle issues. Are they quick to respond to feedback? Do they incorporate professionalism and politeness in their responses? These are the areas guests look out for when renting an Airbnb unit. Such qualities show that you are a good host – one who is willing to accept criticism and enforce improvement.

Optimizing Negative Reviews

As an Airbnb host, you have to respond to both positive and negative reviews to enhance your rental services. To some individuals, bad feedback is synonymous with an extrajudicial execution – one they dread so much. However, this doesn't have to be the case. A good host sees such reviews for what they are – directional signs. They are there to aid one's Airbnb journey. But handling reviews doesn't only revolve around the guidelines discussed above.

Provide a Plan to Improve

Like I stated before, reviews are not meant to cause damage to your Airbnb's business if you are looking in the right places. They are there to make you get better at what you do. A guest may have a problem with a broken showerhead, which may affect the individual's stay in your lodge. As such, there is a likelihood that the person will leave a negative review in that regard when or after checking out. While addressing that feedback, examine the intent. Often, such people want to see improvements when next they check back. You have to let them know that you understand their plights and plan to resolve them immediately.

Whereby there are upgrades, make it a responsibility to update your guests via your listing description and any other communication channel. That way, they know that you place utmost priority on their feedback and are serious about providing them with the best guest experience.

Dwell More on the Brighter Side

Often, when de leave reviews on a listing profile, they cover all the negative aspects of their lodging experience. To use such feedback to your advantage, you have to discuss the positive side of the story as well. But that doesn't imply that you jump right into highlighting how you whipped out $2,300 to replace the TVs in your five rental units or how you spent $35,000 constructing a swimming pool to provide an additional amenity. That will only make you sound cocky.

The first step to take is to acknowledge your mistakes. Once you do that, you've laid the platform on which you can tender your case as well, highlighting several wonderful moments and amenities they enjoyed during their stay. You can wrap your statement up by discussing feasible plans to improve your services immediately. By doing so, your guests will know that you place their comfort first and will most likely check in another time.

Lengthy Responses are Ideal

Chances are unsatisfied guests might drop brief negative reviews on your listing profile. As a newbie, you should not feel dejected; rather, come up with a counter plan, which will not only address the issue but also reduce the severity or impact of the feedback. How can you achieve this? Post a lengthy response. Yes, you heard that right. "How does that help?" you may ask. Here is what you should; lengthy positive responses serve as an ideal cover to mask the impact of a negative review.

Such messages tend to be more detailed and accurate to viewers. Depending on how you present them, they may make you appear as a host who has made efforts to resolve an issue that demands more consideration on the guest's part. This strategy helps you to retain potential travelers in search of rental units. Besides, for you to have taken your time to discuss the problem highlighted by the guest shows that you are willing to make it work.

Make Improvements

It's terrible to make promises you can't keep, especially in business. Nothing hurts one's reputation than this factor.

Like I stated before, genuine guests post negative reviews when they are not satisfied with specific services, with the intent to effect a change. It is up to the host to implement such changes. And like I stated before as well, reviews are directional pointers; they let you know where, when, and how to make adjustments. So, once you have done that, it is ideal to notify your guests about the improvements.

No doubt, positive reviews are great, such that they imply that you are doing a good job. However, if you want to be better at what you do, factor in the negative feedback as well. With that, your business reputation, visibility, and profitability will skyrocket. As a reminder, bad reviews are not there to tarnish your image if you know how to use them to your advantage. And as you handle them, ensure that your services are top-notch to garner more positive reviews and increase your business rating. Here are some highlights on how to boost your rental service reputation:

Promote short-term rentals as more guests will have the platform to post their reviews and ratings

Offer rental discounts from time to time

With these strategies in place, you cannot go wrong in your

Airbnb business.

Resolving Other Challenges Experienced in Airbnb

It is no news that the Airbnb community is growing by leaps and bounds as more potential hosts join the platform and more travelers rent Airbnb units. In other words, the more bookings, the higher the earnings. I presume that you've played your part by understanding specific Airbnb rental laws and codes, acquiring rental vacation property, obtaining necessary permits, taking into account taxes and fees, and many more. Now, you feel all set to start renting your apartment. However, understand that some unforeseen situations are bound to occur, which you should prepare to handle. They may stem from your acquired property or even your guests. If not handled properly, such Airbnb-related problems may set you back tens or hundreds of thousands of dollars. In this section, I have highlighted such potential challenges:

Airbnb pre-check-in issues

Airbnb stay-in issues

In each section, there are solutions to address the challenges, which can save you tons of money. So, let's get into it.

Airbnb Pre-Check-In Issues

Here, I will be discussing challenges you may encounter before an Airbnb guest lodge in your rental apartment.

Late Lodging Duration

According to Benjamin Franklin, "Failing to plan is planning to fail." This quote applies to all activities, including Airbnb services. Of course, you have to prepare for your guest's arrival. However, there are situations where a traveler arrives before the check-in date or stays longer than the allocated booking period. Such activities don't sit right with your Airbnb rental model. For this reason, you have to notify them of available booking changes that you can accept – maybe, precise timeframes opened for modification before and after lodgement. If that is not okay, you can inform them about the unavailability of check-in and check-out adjustments.

Perhaps, you've included such notifications on your listing property profile but still get requests contradicting your rental business schedule; you can decline them politely. Often, such individuals will agree to your terms. However, if you can bear the financial effects that come with their agreements, you can create room for them.

Canceling a Reservation Before Check-In

Not every reservation will see the light of day, based on several factors. In truth, canceling a reservation is simpler than you think, but you have to weigh your options properly and see if house rules, booking policies, damage deposits, home insurance, and the rest are enough to keep your rental apartment safe. Do you know why? According to Airbnb, there are penalties imposed on reservation cancellations. This policy might affect your guest's journey. You can cancel the reservations based on extenuating circumstances.

Late Reservation Cancellation on the Guest's Part

Having an impromptu cancellation can sound like a bombshell to you — it happens sometimes. To prevent this problem from arising, you can set a strict cancellation policy on your listing profile. What does this do? Guests can cancel their reservations at least 14 days to the check-in date. "Won't this affect my occupancy rate?" you may ask. Some Airbnb hosts have had no problem implementing this policy.

Airbnb Stay-In Issues

What if you scale the first phase successfully and they arrive, but things are becoming awry on your property? You may consider resolving this issue. But what problems are likely to surface? Let's find out.

Damaged Amenities

Sometimes, home accessories may break down before the guests arrive. They may include broken showers, loosed doors, and other related problems. Of course, they will not be happy to meet such issues. As such, you should apologize, notify them ahead of time, and promise to resolve it immediately. Kindly tell them to inform you of problems that arise during their stays so that you will not be caught unawares when they leave.

Noisy Neighbors

There is a possibility of you living amid noisy neighbors – you are not to be blamed for such an outcome. Nevertheless, you have to ensure that they have an amazing guest experience. In this case, request that your neighbors keep the noise level to the barest minimum or ideal point. But if such activities reoccur, you may have to reconsider operating an Airbnb business within such an area. You have to fix this problem to prevent a barrage of negative reviews, which may affect your business.

Tension Between Guest/Guest or Guest/Host

Let's assume that your guests are not getting along with each other or one another, or they dislike the host, you may have to step in (if it is necessary). You should not be biased in your approach towards the affected parties. Ensure that they find common ground. On the other hand, if they dislike you (or vice-versa), keep things polite and professional. Such rules of etiquette will help you to run your Airbnb business smoothly.

Kindly keep things cordial between you and your guests, with set boundaries. For misappropriate behavior, you can give them a cautionary note the first time. Although, this is dependent on the severity of the situation. But if such actions repeat themselves, you can request them to vacate your property. Before you take this step, make sure that it is worth it. If you can resolve the problem without canceling the booking, kindly proceed.

Dealing with Partygoers

While running your Airbnb business, you may come across guests that are around for fun. Probably, your vacation home is a top tourist destination. If you are the party-type and are cool with such activities happening on your property, you can give your guests the green light. But you should ensure that they abide by your set rules. In contrast, you may not be such a person. As such, you should address the issue. One of the things you may not accommodate is guests turning your property into a frat house. On this note, you can evict them by canceling the booking.

While you do that, make sure that the necessary documents are in place, should the situation get out of hand. If it is not severe, you can notify them about maintaining decorum throughout their stay, for your sake and that of your neighbor.

Airbnb Post-Check-Out Issues

After your guests may have checked-out, you discovered some things are out of place. How do you handle such an issue? In this section, I will discuss such problems and their solutions; so, don't go anywhere.

Damaged Amenities

This section is where a security deposit comes into play, especially when the damage is on a small scale. You may come back to find out that your tumblers are broken; such deposits will cover the costs. If you have valuable items, like pieces of art, jewelry, and other related items, you need a separate insurance policy.

Misplaced or Stolen Items

Whereby your items are missing (kitchen cutlery set, bed linen, towels, and even artwork), you can ask politely if they have seen them. Make sure that you have searched your property thoroughly before making accusations. You wouldn't want your guests to think that you set them up during their stay. Such an outcome can hamper your business. If they are nowhere to be found, you can file a complaint. On the other hand, if such items are less valuable, notify them without pressing charges. In all, I suggest that you store all valuable items in a different location, maybe a safe deposit box.

Handling Bad Reviews

One of the problems you may face as an Airbnb host is receiving genuine negative reviews from guests that have had bad experiences in your rental units. In response to such feedback, you have to tender a good-hearted apology and notify them of how you plan to fix the issue. Be sure to respond to all reviews as it shows that you care.

In summary, understanding the Airbnb market and its potential challenges can give you an edge over your competitors. But it doesn't stop there; you have to prepare for such unexpected events at all times. This move will help you prevent unfortunate outcomes that might hamper your rental business. And when such events occur, the best thing to do is to stay calm before handling them amicably. As such, you work your way up to becoming a successful host.

How You Can Expand Your Real Estate Properties Via Airbnb

Airbnb hosting provides a unique business platform that may seem different from that of real estate. However, on closer inspection, you will notice that there are several similarities than you initially imagined. This vacation rental hub can help you to build a solid real estate career. As the industry expands, more hosts gravitate towards short-term rentals via vacation housing. Undoubtedly, this strategy guarantees a consistent monthly cash flow. I will point out here that Airbnb has more to offer as it is a new concept in the real estate world even though it has been around for more than a decade. More implementations are on their way, which means that you have more room to expand your rental business.

Before the advent of Airbnb, the real estate market was solely within the confines of realtors. As such, other individuals had limitations exploring this industry. However, this is not the case anymore as anyone can start a rental business, even with a single bed. Investors and real estate agencies now have more avenues to generate more income. Why is that so? About 25% of travelers use the Airbnb rental service at least once, and this number is growing yearly. It means that with an Airbnb rental property, you have the potential to tap into Airbnb's large market share. In other words, you can earn a decent living, leasing your home to guests. In New York City alone, one-third of bookings were solely Airbnb-based short-term rentals. Most travelers need rental spaces that offer them a home-away-from-home experience.

If you have a mortgage on your property and find it challenging to cover it, the Airbnb rental online marketplace is a great start. You don't have to lose your home to your lender with this rental business. All you need are strategies that will help you to generate sustainable sales. And speaking of that, there are several ways to go about it, some of which I have discussed in previous sections. As a reminder, Airbnb is not solely about renting – it transcends this subject. It is more about providing a culture, one which travelers can enjoy. Thankfully, most millennials that are into this business are thinking in that direction. They understand the value of owning and running an Airbnb exclusive property. As a result, they have no problem generating consistent income.

In a situation where you have a property that you find difficult selling, you can convert it into an Airbnb rental unit in the meantime. Potential investors can lodge in such rental vacation homes within a specified timeframe. Once they are satisfied with their stay, it becomes easy for you to pitch your sales idea to them. On the other hand, you may have more time at your disposal to run a rental business with your property. That means more money, which is a smart move. And if that is not the case, you can still sell such units to potential buyers, provided that they are in an attractive location.

Often, property buyers already have plans for the accommodations they intend to purchase. But if that is not the case with yours, you can set up Airbnb accounts for them to manage. As a reminder, potential profit generation revolves around the following:

Highly captivating images

Catchy listing descriptions, and

Other marketing strategies

But, in my opinion, nothing beats running an Airbnb business yourself. It is one way to create an additional income stream and master the real estate industry.

Are There Setbacks?

Everything in life has its merits and demerits, and Airbnb rental is no different from the rest. If you are building a real estate career with this online marketplace, you should be aware of specific challenges, including lucrativeness. Generating consistent returns on your Airbnb investment depends on one main factor – location. In actuality, you can expect more income generation if your property is situated in a top-tourist destination or a high-activity area. Such places are not devoid of significant visits throughout the year.

Also, bear in mind that city codes and laws may affect how you run your Airbnb rental business and, in return, earn a living. Let's go back to New York for a second. Over there, there are attempts to limit what an Airbnb property owner can accomplish. So far, such acts have been futile. Nevertheless, no one knows what the future holds in this regard. To be on the safer side, it is essential to keep abreast of the latest happenings in the real estate industry. With the right marketing strategy, you can expand your real estate business. And if you don't have the technical know-how on this subject matter, hiring an experienced property manager or seeking Airbnb's assistance will do justice.

Chapter 7: The Impact of Property Location on Your Listing

Just as Walmart is known for its one-stop-shopping and everyday low price (EDLP) business strategy, so is Airbnb, also known for its flexible "sharing economy." This online rental marketplace has carved a niche for itself in the hospitality industry by providing guests with a homestay and unique experience. With Airbnb, you get to view the world through the eyes of a local. As such, this rental business has built a strong connection between hosts and guests. But how did it all start? It is worth noting that Airbnb was created to resolve a problem. Joe Gebbia, Airbnb's co-founder, has this to say:

> *Airbnb was born out of necessity. Our rent kept going up. It was born out of a problem.*

With this point in mind, the Airbnb community has witnessed tremendous growth as there are over three million listings in more than 191 countries. And that is not all. This robust rental/cultural platform has birthed more than 650,000 hosts, including myself. Top tourist destinations continue to enjoy the potential profitability this business brings, including the United States, the United Kingdom, Spain, Italy, France, and even some parts of Asia. About 98% of the world's countries promote this service, which means that you can always find a place to stay wherever you are.

Like I stated before, location is everything. And Airbnb uses this element to promote scalability, cultural values, and improved guest experience. Speaking of location, I bet that you may not have come across the name "Bir Billing." To most individuals, some places are left unknown – these are locations that attract tourism and, in turn, can promote an individual's rental business. For example, do you know that Bir Billing exists? This small village is situated in India, and it provides interesting activities, like camping, paragliding, mountain biking, hang gliding, and many more. Not many people will be privy to such a local experience. However, Airbnb bridges such gaps by providing locations based on activities, experiences, and other parameters.

But how does this work? You may have heard of something called "listing quality score." This evaluation metric displays locations based on proximity to a search and review. In other words, the robust platform offers locations through the eyes and voices of guests. With such implementation in view, location can play an essential role in property listings. Via location data, listings can have a better search ranking, such that it becomes easy for guests to find the ideal place for their interests. Remember that I stated before that Airbnb provides smart search; this is not your regular electronic billboard or shopping site. Guests can connect with the right hosts to get the best experience, thanks to streamlined filters, like:

Visibility

Smart pricing

Conversion trigger

Where other property listings are booked within a specific location, other available listings will pop up. Most Airbnb property owners view this rental business as a side gig and not their primary occupation. You may have an extra home that is not in use and decide to make an additional income from it.

Unlike the traditional hospitality platform, guests on Airbnb stay 2.4 times longer than the average hotel lodger. Furthermore, they also spend 2.3 times more than such individuals. As such, most people find this business highly lucrative. I did mention smart pricing as one of the filters used in building a connection. So, let's discuss that in a bit. This part influences profitability. However, it is depending on other sub-elements like:

Responsiveness

Market analysis

Proper investment strategy

Demand fluctuations based on seasonality

With smart pricing, hosts can set optimal rates any time and any day. As conditions change, booking prices change as well in real-time. Back to location, this element affects smart pricing and booking.

Being a part of the "sharing economy," one component you can't forfeit is "trust," as it is the foundation on which all other activities stand. Airbnb understands this and has incorporated it into their business model via the following:

Transparency

Safety

Support

As such, there is trust between guests and hosts. And even when identifying and addressing certain risk factors associated with property listings, the online marketplace considers both behavioral and predictive analytics. This analysis can be in the form of guest screening. Airbnb ensures that travelers who intend to rent Airbnb apartments don't have previous criminal records for the hosts' safety.

According to Brian Chesky,

I'm not saying that the whole world will work this way. But with Airbnb, people are sleeping in other people's homes and other people's beds. So, there is a level of trust necessary to participate that's different from an eBay or Facebook.

This statement shows that the Airbnb community is built on trust. Hosts with good reviews tend to have more bookings and reservations. Even though your rental vacation is situated in an ideal location, trust should be your watchword. Interestingly, Airbnb is building a connection globally via cartography. "But we already have Google, Foursquare, and the likes doing that," you may say. Of course, they are playing their roles significantly. However, Airbnb isn't solely mapping the world; they are building interconnecting relationships as well.

Thanks to Airbnb Maps, it is easy to monitor real-time activities anywhere in the world. What do I mean by this? While relaxing on your sofa, you can view someone riding across the 105-mile scenic bike lane in Milwaukee, Wisconsin, or someone checking in at a luxury Airbnb apartment in Albuquerque, New Mexico. The standard maps don't provide a list of culturally inclined locations. So, you may have no idea where to visit to get the best experience. However, Airbnb addresses this issue via mapping. Hence, guests don't have a problem visiting attractive tourist spots.

When running this large rental business hub, there are chances that certain locations will be bugged with over-tourism. For this reason, the company promotes even distribution and geographic diversity. About 72% to 93% of listings sit on locations that are outside the traditional tourist zones. As such, there is less concentration in such areas. Surprisingly, the traditional hospitality sector does not provide this option. Additionally, reviews and ratings give Airbnb guests an idea of what to expect when moving to a new location.

But Airbnb isn't only about guests, in case you are wondering. Hosts also get to enjoy increased booking conversion – thanks to Airbnb's top-notch matching algorithms.

Conclusion

We have covered almost everything that has to do with Airbnb and real estate. But for the sake of clarity, I will run through some of the topics in this section. Like I stated before, Airbnb rental business provides hosts with the platform to generate additional income streams while offering guests ideal accommodations. But remember that not everyone will find this robust online rental marketplace suitable. If you choose to continue with your real estate adventure, you have to understand the risks and rewards. This statement brings us back to this question again. What is Airbnb investing?

When you talk or think about Airbnb investing, see it as a strategy that offers rental investment to investors and other stakeholders. You don't need to rent out your entire living space to be in this business. If you have multiple properties that are not in use, this is a perfect opportunity to generate significant cash flow. Airbnb is not the only property listing platform out there. I have pointed others as well, including VRBO. You can compare listing sites to find out the ideal option for your rental business.

Another area I have addressed is business profitability. Many of you that are new to Airbnb are wondering if it is profitable. If you are looking at the investment side of this platform, then I will say yes. That does not mean that there are no drawbacks. However, you have to prepare for such outcomes. So, what are the pros and cons of Airbnb? Let's start by discussing the benefits.

With Airbnb, you are guaranteed an additional income stream and cash flow. Each day, travelers are looking for available rental accommodations. With the right image and description, you can implore them to take action on your listing. Also, keep in mind that location is important. If run properly, you can give hotels a run for their money. Find out how they treat and charge guests and use such a cue to your advantage.

Kindly note that maintaining an Airbnb is simpler than running a traditional rental service. You may be wondering if this is possible. If you are operating short-term rentals, your property will be in optimum shape at all times. And guess what? You are not the one covering the cleaning cost – your guests are. Cleaning fees can range from $75 to $200, depending on the host. It is also easy to identify problems that may arise on the property.

Are there downsides to this business? Of course, yes. For those individuals seeking passive investment, this robust online marketplace may not offer the best deal. Like I stated before, Airbnb is not a billboard. You have to keep your profile and listing alive to achieve success. Every process in this business does not evade your attention. And if you can't handle this business, you can hire a property manager. Do not forget the risks as well. Some hosts may view this as a demerit, and others overlook it. Depending on your take on this subject matter, there is no denying that Airbnb rental business has its risks, which may cost you your property or finance. As such, you have to consider the risk factors I discussed in this guide.

Profiting from Airbnb

Airbnb is a profitable business if you have an investment strategy in place. However, take note that there is no one-size-fits-all technique when running this rental business. You have to factor in your short and long-term goals and see how they align with the business model. I have stated before ways you can run a profitable Airbnb. But here is the summary:

Research the Airbnb location. Is it a desirable place that has the potential to fetch you returns on investment? How close is your potential property to landmarks and amenities? Is there easy freeway access? These are questions worth asking. Location determines how you set your nightly rates.

Understand dynamic pricing. You don't want to fizzle out of the market due to under-priced or overpriced booking. You have to know what the rental sector is saying per time. What are your competitors charging guests on any day? Embrace market demand in relation to pricing.

Don't shy away from charging extra for additional amenities. If your guests need more than the standard, they should be able to cover the costs, no questions asked. This is business, and you are in charge. As much as you are running your

Airbnb to provide them with the best guest experience, you also in it to earn a living. So, play your cards right.

Maximizing Such Profits

If you don't have a property for Airbnb, you might have to get one. And this cost money. Even if you do have one, you may need to renovate it – another expense as well. As such, you have to know how to balance your expenditures and earnings to optimize profits. The rental business is one of the most profitable ventures out there. But very few people know how to tap into the infinite rewards of this platform. So, let me show you the way.

Treat your rental as a business. It is not uncommon to find Airbnb newbies making the mistake of running their rental homes like a charity organization. Of course, it is good to be nice. But remember, you are in this to not only satisfy your guests but also generate cash flow. There are needs to be met. And if you reside in an apartment that is owned by a landlord, such an individual will not give you a listening ear when the rent is due. Do you want to be successful in your Airbnb business? Run it like you will run a hotel. Provide optimum services that will give guests value for their money.

Numbers don't lie. Is Airbnb worth the try? You may ask. First, run through the numbers and see if they add up as expected. If you have several properties, you can experiment with one and see the results. In doing so, consider time and effort, occupancy rates, available rental options, and management. These factors and many more will help you decide on running your Airbnb business full time.

Creativity is everything. Do you want guests to be interested in your property? Come up with strategies that will capture their attention. Create professional and captivating property listing photographs. Your rental unit décor must also be on point, such that guests always come back. Don't forget the place of artwork.

Identify your audience. Who do you want on your property? Are you after high-paying guests? Or do you want to cater to modest Airbnb travelers? Is your property built to provide a luxury experience? Or do you want to compete with other Airbnb hosts within your vicinity? These factors will help you put all things in place. Tailor your business to suit your guests' personalities.

In summary, you can earn a sustainable living with Airbnb. But before you start seeing returns, make sure that you have identified the merits and demerits, business goals, investment strategies, and other elements. As you run your rental business, you gather more experience to provide your guests with the best satisfaction.

Appendix 1: Rental Property Apps Worth Trying

As the real estate market becomes highly competitive, guests are seeking rental accommodations that serve as their next homes. As such, properties are available one moment and unavailable the next. Ideal renting is heating up by the day. Nevertheless, these individuals can find accurate listings through smart search options, thanks to the sophisticated online rental listing sector. Apps are available to provide detailed rental information on the fly, which has created a seamless workflow. Here are some of them:

Apartments.com

Zillow rentals

Rent.com

HotPads

Trulia Rentals

Zumper

Realtor.com Rentals

Apartments by Apartment Guide

Apartments Finder

RadPad

Why do you need these apps? In truth, not everyone has the time to hunt for rental homes. Besides, it may take forever to find the ideal unit amid millions of listing properties. These rental apps come in handy during such moments. While waiting at the train station, you could check out the next available listing vacation apartment. Everything you need is at your fingertip. In the words of Jeremy Wacksman (Zillow's President), "Today people expect magic at the touch of a button, and finding their next home is no exception." He goes on to say this, "Renters have told us they want the entire rental process to happen online, which is why we've made it possible to complete an application, obtain a credit check, apply for a rental, and pay rent – all from our app.

There's tons of opportunity to make the process even better, but these new features are a big step forward in making renting, buying, and selling a home a more seamless, on-demand experience." There is no denying that rental apps are bridging the gap in the real estate market.

One of the notable apps, Zumper, provides a platform for guests to submit their information, including credit reports, before exploring listing properties. There is a secure system for them to forward their application easily. According to the CEO, Anthemos Georgiades, "Our mission is to make renting an apartment as easy as booking a hotel." That being stated, let us discuss the listed apps. Note: these apps are android- and IOS-based.

Apartments.com:

You can come across the android or IOS version of this map-based app. Apartments.com offers renters real-time property availability, not leaving behind amenities and charges. On this app, they can view available vacation homes in 3D before visiting them in person.

Zillow Rentals:

Also available on Android and IOS, Zillow Rentals avail

renters of over 400,000 rental units within the country. And you know what? This app allows you to personalize your search using specific parameters, like:

On-site parking

Pet policy

In-unit laundry, and many more

Renters can save the results generated from such filters. Another feature you can't ignore on this app is the automatic payment system for online rentals. There may be a charge for this process, depending on the payment type. They can also furnish several landlords with information within 30 days for a fee of $29. These include eviction records, Experian credit reports, and background checks.

Rent.com:

Like the two previously discussed apps, this mobile platform lets you take a tour of interesting properties and search for open visit times. But that is not all; you can also streamline your property search based on reviews through a residential survey system.

HotPads:

If you are looking for property listings based on top cities in a country, HotPads is the ideal app. With this Android/IOS-based application, you can narrow your search to include features surrounding the location you intend to rent an apartment in at any time. There is also room for hot listing searches to get the best rental apartment.

Trulia Rentals:

With Trulia Rentals, you are one click away from finding an ideal property manager to consult on any property of interest. You don't have to hunt property owners' contact details or fill an inquiry form to get the information you seek.

Zumper:

This robust mobile app provides renters with more than a million rental listings. Set notification for any apartment that catches your fancy and receive an alert when it is available. With Zumper, you can also submit your Experian credit report to as many landlords as you can reach. If you reside in cities where the rental space is highly competitive, you can use features, like:

Prequalification

Booking tours

Rental offer proposals

Realtor.com Rentals:

If you want to search for available properties through images and maps, the Realtor.com app is the right way to go. And whereby you intend to check out such rental accommodations in person, the mobile application gives you driving directions. You also receive alerts on properties that match your requirements before contacting a leasing agency all through the same mobile platform.

Apartments by Apartment Guide:

Are you looking for floor plans and images of interesting properties for rent? Apartments by Apartment Guide app is your go-to rental companion. You can save and share property listings on the go.

Apartments Finder:

If you are renting for the first time and are conscious of your expenses, you would want to look at the Apartments Finder app. With this Android/IOS app, you can easily find ideal properties that match your budget, including those that come with the following:

Short-term housing

Housing vouchers

Utilities

RadPad:

Nationwide property listings are available on RadPad. There is an online rental payment option that comes either through debit or credit financing. Once the renter has made a payment, the company forwards it to the landlord.

Appendix 2: Investing in Other Related Jobs

The real estate market is dynamic. Several moving parts are constantly in motion. As such, many careers are in high demand. In the United States, there are about two million active real estate licensees. So, if you are not particular about the traditional white-collar jobs, this is an avenue for you to build a career in this field. In actuality, some of these opportunities are not known to many people, even though they are highly lucrative. And even if they are, you may find it mind-boggling to choose the right career path. I recommend that you start by researching what you want in the real estate sector. Here is a list of real estate-related jobs worth trying.

Home Inspector:

The role of a home inspector is to evaluate available properties for flaws that may affect sales, rentals, or management. Such inspections are essential to ensure that buyers and sellers conduct seamless transactions. As a home inspector, you have to identify defects that may be inconspicuous to the average person. According to

Glassdoor, such a role comes with an average annual income of $38,000.

How do you become a home inspector? This factor depends on your state of residence. If you live in cities like California, you don't need a license to practice this occupation. But bear in mind that intensive training is essential to become a professional home inspector. What other requirements are inclusive? You need to be well-versed in the following:

Plumbing

Wall structure

Roofing

Electricity and other related fields

I recommend that you don't jump into this field without having the right training.

Real Estate Broker:

It is easy to assume that a real estate broker and agent

perform the same task. To an extent, their roles are similar, but looking at it beyond the surface, both professionals work for different bodies. Interestingly, the latter works for the former since the individual signs with a brokerage. As a real estate broker, you can create your brokerage or work independently as an entrepreneur. Find which of the career options works best for you. What requirements are needed to become a real estate broker?

First, I will state that there are state laws. In general, you need a minimum of a year of working experience as a real estate agent before you can process a broker license application. You have to undergo a training course and real estate broker licensing exam as well. Once you've cleared both requirements, you can enjoy a prosperous career in the real estate industry. Individuals in this field earn an average annual income of $72,500.

Real Estate Wholesaler:

Another top career that is available in the real estate sector is real estate wholesaling. This field involves:

Locating distressed properties that are available for quick sales

Initiating such sales and contract signings

Searching for a buyer to sell available properties for profits

Evaluating renovation requirements and after repair value (ARV) of properties

It is worth mentioning that real estate wholesaling does not entail a fix-and-flip approach – that is, a different career path entirely. Let me explain them in detail. A real estate flipper purchases and renovates distressed homes before selling them to buyers, whereas a real estate wholesaler doesn't. They provide investors with statistics showing the renovation costs and ARV, which will initiate a CTA.

And guess what? You don't need all the money in the world to get started with this career. You can venture into the real estate industry without breaking the bank. All you need is to look out for distressed units and be able to negotiate deals effectively. As I have stated in other sections, don't expect overnight success. Gradually build your way up.

Real Estate Agent:

This career is popular in the real estate sector. Perchance, you have come across thousands of professionals in this field. But what do they do? It's simple, and I bet you already know the answer as well. They aid in the purchase and sales of properties. It implies that you may focus on either buying properties or selling them. There are two types of real estate agents:

Residential agent

Commercial agent

The first type of agent deals with residential units. They ensure smooth transactions of purchases on available homes between buyers and sellers. And if you want to narrow the area of expertise further, other elements come into play, including property type. A residential agent can focus solely on any of the following:

Condos

Single-family homes

Vacation homes

Luxury apartments

Foreclosures

To become a residential real estate agent, one of the prerequisites required of you is to own a license. But to run a sustainable career, it is essential to provide clients with optimum satisfaction. And these include having unique customer service, marketing skills, networking skills, and lead generation tactics in place. Let's move on to the second option.

A commercial real estate agent's role is not different from that of a residential real estate agent. But this time around, the individual focuses solely on the commercial aspect of the real estate sector. What do I mean? Professionals in this field provide businesses with real estate properties. As such, they have to be well-versed in business and finance. As a commercial real estate agent, you will be dealing with the following:

Capitalization rates

Gross rent multipliers

Internal rates of return

Income generation on real estate agencies is on a commission basis. So, your earnings are dependent on the volume of transactions conducted. For this reason, you have to understand how to generate leads and seal more deals. Commercial real estate agents tend to earn more than their counterparts.

Property Manager:

There are real estate investors, and there are property managers. The former may have no time to manage their investment properties, even though they earn passively from it. As such, they can hire the latter to help them oversee all activities concerning property management. If your interest lies in this field, you have to ensure that the home in question is in good shape, both physically and financially. Additionally, renters' satisfaction is of utmost priority. You will be liaising with both parties to ensure that everything is in optimum performance. However, delving into property management requires you to have a broker license. Other skills include:

Problem-solving

Managerial skills

Customer service

Marketing

Accounting

Documentation

As a property manager, you are expected to earn an average annual income of $54,000.

Real Estate Developer:

This career is an interesting one. Why do I say so? Imagine building a property from scratch. You can purchase a piece of land and construct anything you want on it, ranging from a two-bedroom apartment to an office complex. It doesn't end there; you have to oversee the construction of such buildings. These include team coordination and financing. Real estate developers work with other professionals, like:

Contractors

Engineers

Architects

Construction workers

Lawyers

Leasing agents, just to mention a few

Unlike other real estate professions discussed above, real estate development requires a minimum of a four-year degree program in any of the following:

Architecture

Civil engineering

Business real estate

Urban planning

And not only that, but you also have to be well-versed in the following areas:

Planning process

Multitasking

Real estate market

Project management

Interpersonal communications

Finances, and

The economy as a whole

Income generation in this career path is dependent on several factors, including the property type in question, the company in charge of the project, and your years of experience.

Real Estate Investor:

The most gratifying profession you can embark on in the real estate industry is real estate investment. There is less work involved in this sector if you know how to play your cards right. You need to know when and where to purchase investment properties and sell them to maximize profits. This strategy involves you understanding the real estate market and its moving parts. It is worth stating that this career path doesn't solely center on transactions. Remember, you will be taking a huge risk all the time. Hence, you don't want to find yourself on the losing side. So, what are the qualities required of you?

Capital – you need money to get started with this career.

You must be willing to take calculated risks

Have a keen eye for promising investment properties with good ROI

Know when and how to implement investment strategies, including fix-and-flip, buy-and-hold, rentals, and many more

You have to find out which property type will be ideal for your business, whether residential or commercial

I mentioned before that you need money to start a real estate investment, but that doesn't imply that you have to empty your life savings. With the right strategy in place, you can invest in a property and generate passive income. Robert T. Kiyosaki is a perfect example of a real estate investor. I recommend that you read his books. The earnings in this field are limitless and mind-blowing. According to ZipRecruiter, some of these individuals rake in an average annual income of $124,000.

Real Estate Consultant:

Once you have built a sustainable career in any of the fields I have discussed so far, you can decide to venture into real estate consultancy. As a consultant, you have to provide companies or real estate investors with in-depth information on real estate investment. Financially speaking, such consultations can fetch the individual an average annual income of $67,000. You can easily spot real estate market trends, which will help investors to make the right decision to achieve their investment goals. However, to venture into this career, you need a license.

Real Estate Attorney:

Real estate attorneys are there to provide legalities that address property disputes. Such issues may stem from the following:

Transfers

Documentation

Title

As a real estate attorney, you have to guide clients through any real estate transaction process and ensure that it is legit. Where there are legal issues, you should diffuse the tension. Like a real estate developer, professionals in this field need a Bachelor's degree. They also have to earn a Juris Doctor degree. Other examinations to pass include the bar exam and law school admission test (LSAT). Generally, real estate attorneys may spend six to eight years and an additional two years as a lawyer before being allowed to practice this career. Interestingly, the annual income is lucrative. According to Glassdoor, you should expect an average yearly take-home pay of $119,000.

Mortgage Broker:

If you have a knack for interpersonal relations and figures, mortgage brokerage may offer an opportunity for you to build a successful career. Such professionals are the middlemen between lenders and borrowers. But does this center only around money? Not at all. They evaluate mortgage loan products as well. Their expertise encapsulates the following:

Qualification requirements

Loan availability

Terms and conditions

Interest rates and many more

Becoming a mortgage broker is no walk in the park. The following comes into play:

SAFE Mortgage Loan Originator Test

Pre-licensing mortgage broker training

Mortgage broker bond

Mortgage broker licensing

Professional network building

More studies on mortgage lending

As a mortgage broker, you can earn an average annual income of $51,000.

Real Estate Appraiser:

Real estate appraisers "appraise" or evaluate a real estate property's value based on location, features, and other competing properties. Such real estate can be residential or commercial. However, becoming a professional in this field requires you to have an appraiser's license. You can easily get this, unlike some careers I discussed in this section. All you need is to undergo a 75-hour training program on the fundamental aspect of this field and pass the state exam. You may also need education in finance and economics. Interestingly, you can work as an entrepreneur or partner with a large corporation. Your potential average annual take-home pay sits at $53,000.

Real Estate Loan Officer:

The title accurately defines the rule of this career. Professionals in this field are responsible for providing clients with loan procuring opportunities. They help clients with specific budget sizes to purchase properties. To become a practicing official, you have to register with the Nationwide Mortgage Licensing System. There are requirements for this as well. You also need to be well-versed in finance. As a real estate loan officer, your average annual income hovers around $34,000.

These are some of the real estate career paths you can venture into and make a decent living. Commencing with any of them will create more opportunities for you to explore the real estate sector and generate more passive income. Some of these professions demand that you have a license and a relevant degree, while others require extensive training. Find out which one works for you best.

www.ingramcontent.com/pod-product-compliance
Lightning Source LLC
Chambersburg PA
CBHW070336220526
45467CB00001B/146